Department of English Local History
OCCASIONAL PAPERS
Fourth Series   Edited by Charles Phythian-Ada
Number 4

Hanbury: *Settlement and Society in a Woodland Landscape*

CHRISTOPHER DYER
Reader in Medieval History,
University of Birmingham

LEICESTER UNIVERSITY PRESS 1991

First published in Great Britain in 1991 by Leicester University Press
(a division of Pinter Publishers Ltd)
© Christopher Dyer 1991

Editorial offices
Fielding Johnson Building, University of Leicester,
University Road, Leicester, LE1 7RH

Trade and other enquiries
25 Floral Street, London, WC2E 9DS

British Library Cataloguing in Publication Data

A CIP cataloguing record for this book is available
from the British Library

ISBN 0-7185-2037-8

Front cover: Church Hill, Hanbury (Worcestershire), from the south-east.
Photo by R. Swift

The author acknowledges the generous assistance of the
Marc Fitch Fund.

Contents

List of figures

List of tables

Acknowledgements

The research for this paper has involved more than a hundred people, and it is not possible to thank all of them here by name. Members of three successive extra-mural classes held at Hanbury helped to transcribe documents and to collate medieval and modern topographical information. Students from the School of History of the University of Birmingham surveyed the fields of the parish. These two pieces of work form the basis of much of the interpretation of Hanbury's landscape history presented here. Encouragement and practical help for the extra-mural classes came from staff of the Birmingham department, Philip Barker, Robin Chaplin, Kevin Down and Graham Martin. Philippa Bassett made the county record office available to the class and advised us on the modern documents. The field-work was based on Hanbury Hall, and the use of rooms there was provided by Selby Clewer on behalf of the National Trust. The landowners of the parish gave permission for their land to be surveyed and field-walked. Special thanks are due to Mr A. Terry of Hownings Farm and Mr Few of Ditchford Bank who informed us of their own finds. News of archaeological discoveries in the parish also came from Jan Roberts (then of Hereford and Worcester County Council), David Symons of Birmingham City Museum, and W.A. Seaby. Identifications of archaeological material were made by Donald Mackreth, Edwina Proudfoot, Alan Saville and Derek Simpson. Paul Booth and Alan Vince commented on the pottery. Grenville Astill, Mick Aston, Lawrence Barfield and Simon Esmonde Cleary gave general archaeological advice and encouragement. Susan Limbrey provided expertise on the soils. Margaret Gelling interpreted the place-names. Jim Berrow provided flights in his light aircraft. Air photographs were also examined from the Cambridge collection (by courtesy of Professor J.K. St Joseph) and the RAF sorties in the care of the Royal Commission on Historical Monuments (England). Historical information came from Wendy Davies and Stephen Price. Ron Swift and Graham Norrie helped with photographs. John West allowed the use of information from his unpublished M.A. thesis. Andrew Harris gave constant help, hospitality and encouragement. Steven Bassett helped to organize the survey of earthworks. He has been a constant source of ideas, and will publish the results of his own researches into the area.

Financial help came from the Field Research Fund of the University of Birmingham, and the Marc Fitch Fund which made a grant towards the cost of the illustrations. Harold Fox and Charles Phythian-Adams encouraged the publication of the research as a Leicester Occasional Paper, and Harold Fox was an attentive and sympathetic editor.

This paper has three aims: first to extend our general knowledge of the development of the English landscape and settlement pattern; second to encourage others to embark on similar projects, both for the academic benefits, and because of the need to record the evidence before its destruction; and third to inform the people of north Worcestershire about the history of their countryside, which is currently under threat.

Christopher Dyer, School of History, University of Birmingham   *June 1990*

Chapter 1

Introduction

THE PROBLEM

'Settlement' has two meanings for the local historian; the occupation of land in general, and a site for dwellings in a village, hamlet or farm. Previous Leicester Occasional Papers have been concerned with settlement in both senses, because some have explored the past use of tracts of the countryside at Withington, Chippenham, Claybrooke and Wychwood, and others have investigated the deserted villages of Oxfordshire and Northamptonshire.[1] Hanbury follows in these traditions, and indeed seeks to unite the two fields of inquiry. It is not written by a member of the Leicester school of local historians, but by an outsider who has been influenced by their work.

The investigation of Hanbury began, as any research project must, by asking questions. These arose from the rapidly developing knowledge of settlement among archaeologists, geographers and historians. To begin with the rural landscape, great advances have been made in classifying the varieties of countryside. An old distinction between the highland and the lowland zone emphasized the influence of the natural environment on settlement.[2] A more recent but equally simple scheme puts more weight on the human factor by dividing the 'planned' from the 'ancient' countryside, the 'planned' countryside being the regions with nucleated villages and modern enclosure, contrasted with the 'ancient' regions of dispersed settlement and old enclosure.[3] The idea of varied *pays* developed at Leicester does more justice to the complexity of the landscape. Physical and social differences define the character of the feldon or champion countries, the woodlands, the wolds, the fenlands and so on. These were often first recognized by the early county historians such as Dugdale, and can be given more scientific definition from manorial records, estate maps and probate inventories.[4] To take as examples the two main *pays* of the West Midlands, the feldon or champion country lay in the Avon valley and the clay plains of central Worcestershire and south-east Warwickshire. Here in the thirteenth and fourteenth centuries were nucleated villages, open fields and peasants holding standard customary tenements who made their living primarily from corn-growing. In the woodlands of north Warwickshire and north and west Worcestershire the scattered settlements lay among wood and pasture mingled with arable. The fields were irregular and often enclosed. The landholdings were more unequal in size, the inhabitants enjoyed more freedom, and they practised a greater variety of occupations than would be found in the feldon.[5]

Having recognized the patchwork of varying landscapes, more work is still needed to define the boundaries between one *pays* and another, and to examine differences within each type. Woodlands were especially varied: Rockingham Forest in Northamptonshire, for example, included many nucleated villages, which are rare in the Worcestershire woodlands, except for the scatter of important settlements that functioned as market centres.

We also need to learn more about the early history of the *pays*. There is a temptation to note the deeply sunken lanes of the woodlands, or the heavy corrugations of the ridge and furrow of the feldon, and to think that things were ever thus. Now we can contemplate the discovery that the medieval Oxfordshire forests were occupied in the Roman period with fields of corn, and we have known for some time that the now empty parts of the Warwickshire Feldon were once dotted with arable-farming villages, but within a few generations in the period 1380–1520 many square miles were converted to thinly inhabited pastures.[6] *Pays* could change their character radically, and sometimes rapidly.

The other area of inquiry is to explore more deeply the workings of the economy and society of the *pays*. This means research not just into their farming systems, but also into their demographic complexion, their relationship with the market and the influence of lordship.[7] Did regions differ because of inherent qualities of the soil or climate, or because of social institutions or human choice?

To turn to settlements in the narrower sense, their modern study began with deserted villages and moved on to questions of village origins.[8] Now that we know that nucleated villages developed at rather a late stage – from the ninth century (in parts of Northamptonshire) to the twelfth (in County Durham) – dispersed settlements seem all the more important.[9] First, they represent the settlement type that preceded the village, not just in the early Middle Ages but also in prehistoric and Roman times. Second, nucleated villages were confined mainly to a belt of land running through England from Northumberland to the Channel, thus leaving most of the country, including some of its most populous parts, to be classed as non-village regions.[10] And third, we recognize the persistence and longevity of dispersed settlements. They continued into modern times, and even revived when the enclosure movement sent the farms out into the fields, while many villages, seen by some as an aberration in settlement history, survived for only a few centuries.[11]

The classification of dispersed settlements still needs to be considered. We know that the straggling green-edge hamlets of East Anglia differ from the isolated upland farms of Somerset, and that there are many other variations in between.[12] But we have no typology, and no agreed vocabulary to describe and analyse dispersion. In carrying out such an elementary Linnean exercise we cannot focus too narrowly on the buildings, yards and roads of the hamlets and farms but need to see how they functioned within the agrarian landscape.

The social meaning of dispersed settlements is another area of inquiry. The relationship between the manor and the village seems even more complex now that we have learnt that estates originated long before the ninth century, that is before the formation of villages.[13] The fact that some villages are now known to have been laid out in regular plans, and that nucleated villages and regular open-field systems originated at a time of a general ordering of English life, when the state, the towns and the parochial system were all developing, leads some scholars to argue that villages were planned by their lords.[14] Others associate the growth of the coherent village, not with the rise of feudal power directly, but with the emergence of communities as important social and political forces in the high Middle Ages.[15] In either case, it is still instructive to note that some regions were more prone to reorganization of settlements and village planning than others.

Similarly we can learn something about the nature of both the villages and the dispersed settlements from their decline. It is generally accepted that hamlets and farms were abandoned in the fourteenth and fifteenth centuries, but was the scale of the loss greater among the villages? The vulnerability of different communities to crises might tell us about their character in the times of growth.[16]

The study of a single parish cannot answer these critical questions, but it can make a contribution towards their solution. In this case we are concerned first to consider the chronology of settlement. Did the clearance of woods begin in the Middle Ages, or were the woodlands inhabited in prehistory? Was the woodland landscape a product of the Middle Ages or earlier periods? How were woodland settlements organized, how did they work in relation to the agrarian resources and what was the character of woodland society? How did the settlements fare in the contraction of the fourteenth and fifteenth centuries? In decline, as in growth, we must ask if the physical environment determined the economy and settlement of the woodlands or whether lords and the peasant communities in any way decided their own destinies.

HANBURY, AND THE RESEARCH PROJECT

The Worcestershire parish of Hanbury was chosen as the subject of a research programme for a number of reasons. I had spent some years writing the history of the estates of the bishopric of Worcester, of which Hanbury formed a part.[17] A topographical study of the estate had seemed a natural and necessary accompaniment to the documentary research but took up too much time to be achieved in detail – the 17 manors of the estate extended over hundreds of square miles. However, once the main task had been completed, examining the landscape of selected manors could be attempted. Hanbury seemed an ideal first candidate because its settlements did not fit into any simple category. Most of the bishopric manors lay in the Avon and Severn valleys and on the Cotswolds, and contained nucleated villages and hamlets; the inhabitants of Alvechurch, the other north-east Worcestershire manor, lived either in Alvechurch borough or in isolated farms and small hamlets scattered over the parish.[18] Hanbury combined dispersed settlements with hints of nucleation. The church seemed strangely isolated on its hilltop, and earthworks nearby could perhaps mark the site of a former village. In the centre of the parish stood a group of houses around a shop, village hall, and the Vernon Arms public house which the modern inhabitants call 'the village'. The documents referred to a settlement of some size called Blickley, but this was hard to locate as all that survived of the name was a house called Brickley near a few farms and cottages now known as Ditchford Bank. Was this a deserted medieval village? These were small problems, but together they seemed to epitomize the difficulties faced by all historians in attempting to understand the complex settlements of the woodlands. There were also non-academic reasons for choosing Hanbury. It was easily accessible from Birmingham, and although it was surrounded by the three towns of Bromsgrove, Droitwich and Redditch (fig. 1), it had survived as an attractive piece of countryside, including scenic hills on its northern border, and the National Trust property of Hanbury Hall in the west. It even enjoyed a popular reputation as the original setting for *The Archers*, the fictional BBC radio 'everyday story of countryfolk'.[19] This seemed to be an appropriate place to investigate the everyday history of past country dwellers.

Closer acquaintance showed that Hanbury offered a number of advantages for research. A large parish (7,790 acres or 3,155 ha) (12 sq miles or 31 sq km) gives an extensive enough sample of country, comparable with such places as Wharram Percy, Chalton and Raunds, where research has yielded such useful insights into the long-term evolution of settlement.[20] Hanbury's present low population density ensures that earlier field evidence has not been obscured by recent development. Modern mixed farming provides archaeological evidence both in the form of earthworks in pasture fields and scatters of pottery on the arable. The place is well-documented through the survival of the archives of the bishopric of Worcester, partly in the collection of the Church Commissioners, and partly in the muniments of the Vernons of Hanbury Hall. The Vernon manuscripts are especially valuable because the continuous series of records enables individual farms to be traced over centuries, and in particular an estate map and survey, compiled by the distinguished Dougharty family of mapmakers in 1731–2, contains a mass of valuable information. John Dougharty, junior, in 1744 also redrew and thereby preserved a map of Feckenham of 1591 which includes a section of Hanbury omitted from the Vernon map.[21] Other written sources are contained in the archives of the Bearcrofts of Mere Hall, of the Talbots of Grafton Manor, and of Bordesley Abbey. The administration of the royal forest of Feckenham has left us with a mass of plea rolls, perambulations and other records. The emphasis of the project on the reconstruction of the topography of the parish means that the most valuable documents are the surveys, especially a rental of 1466 which listed tenements in topographical sequence, as if the compilers had noted the information as they rode down the lanes. Almost every document contains some topographical information: charters with their descriptions of the location of plots of land, and court rolls and account rolls which describe holdings by the surnames of long-dead tenants (Wyntors, Menskes, Wyghtes and so on), enabling scattered medieval houses to be located on the modern map.

With the help of students in an extra-mural class held in Hanbury, card indexes were compiled of the names of houses, fields, roads, streams and other features mentioned in the medieval records. When the field and other names in the eighteenth and nineteenth-century maps had also been indexed, a sufficient number of names could be matched to enable a map to be prepared of the topography of late medieval Hanbury. This was accomplished with no little difficulty, as the distortion of names sometimes renders them almost unrecognizable, or a name has changed its meaning. For example, the owner of The White House was puzzled because his house is of brick and showed no sign of having been any colour other than red. However, the tenure of the site by the medieval family of Wyght must explain the origin of the modern name. A more intractable problem lies in the uneven survival of records. The southern end of the parish lay in two poorly documented manors, and we are consequently less fully informed about their medieval topography.

In a separate research programme, each field in the parish was visited and recorded by history students as a field-work training exercise. They noted all earthworks, including ridge and furrow and settlement remains. Subsequently some of the better preserved settlement sites were planned. Meanwhile a field-walking programme was carried out, collecting material from a sample of more than a hundred arable fields in the parish. This was supplemented by gathering information about chance finds from museums and local people, which revealed a surprising amount of archaeological material. Air photographs were examined for earthworks and cropmarks, and I twice flew over the parish to search for sites and take photographs. A certain amount of analysis was done on the botanical species in modern hedgerows, but not on a systematic basis. During field-work architectural evidence was noted, and local experts on buildings were consulted, but this was not a very useful source as only one or two medieval vernacular buildings survive in the parish.

The choice of a parish as the unit of study, rather than a sample of kilometre squares, or an area defined by physical geography such as a stream valley, needs some justification. The programme of research is multi-period, but the focus on the Middle Ages and the use of documents makes it very convenient to use manorial and parish boundaries. In one respect the survey was inconsistent in this, because Huntingdrop, originally a detached part of Dodderhill parish and not incorporated into Hanbury until the nineteenth century, was none the less included in the area studied.[22] The use of the parish might imply that the boundary defines an area which had some significance before the Middle Ages, but there is no justification for such a view. The prehistoric and Romano-British inhabitants of Hanbury lived within administrative units of some kind, but their boundaries are not known.

The research programme was designed to recover as much information as possible from every available source. The interpretation of the evidence involves the combination of the skills and methods of historians, archaeologists and geographers.

THE PARISH IN ITS REGION

Hanbury's location in north-east Worcestershire (fig. 1) places it near the edge of the early provinces and kingdoms of the West Midlands. In the late Iron Age and the Roman period it lay on the northern extremity of the territory of the Dobunni, centred on Bagendon (in the Iron Age) and Cirencester in the period of Roman rule.[23] In the seventh and eighth centuries it was sited within the sub-kingdom of the Hwicce, which was gradually absorbed into the larger kingdom of Mercia. The Hwicce's northern boundary is assumed to be preserved in that of the diocese of Worcester, which was also used in the tenth and eleventh centuries to define the northern edge of Worcestershire.[24] At the time of Domesday Hanbury belonged to the hundred of Esch, but later was incorporated into the bishop of Worcester's triple hundred and liberty of Oswaldslow.[25]

An important influence on its development was the proximity of Droitwich, a salt-making centre from the Iron Age until the nineteenth century.[26] The wells of Droitwich yielded brine with a high level of salinity, and after evaporation the finished product was distributed over the West Midlands on a network of salt-ways.[27] Thereby places remote from the coast could obtain conveniently their essential supplies of salt, and Droitwich enjoyed a vital position within the economy of the region. Hanbury was associated with the salt industry in its earliest records: charters of 657–74 and 836 mention salt-pits and lead furnaces (where the brine was boiled), presumably located at Droitwich, as part of the assets of the estate, and in Domesday salt-houses and salt-renders were attached to both the bishop of Worcester's manor of Hanbury and the royal manor of *Holeway*. The administrative link between the bishop's manor and his Droitwich salt-works persisted in the later Middle Ages.[28] For example, in 1391–2 the bailiff of Hanbury manor paid for two buildings from Bradley (to the east of Hanbury) to be dismantled, carried to Droitwich, and re-erected at the salt-house.[29] Hanbury may in early times have had a relationship not merely of association with the salt industry. The early charters mention salt-pits, not just the boiling-houses where the salt was extracted, implying that part of the brine supplies were in some sense managed from Hanbury. It would be tempting to see the Iron Age hill-fort on Church Hill, the only fortification of the period in the vicinity of Droitwich, as having a protective or controlling function in relation to the salt industry, though this role was presumably transferred in the first century AD to the Roman fort at Dodderhill and ultimately to the nearby opulent building in Bays Meadow which might have housed an imperial official or lessee.[30]

If this suggestion of the original purpose of the fort on Church Hill is thought to be too speculative, there can be no question of the hilltop's importance as the administrative centre of a large rural area over many centuries. Coins from Church Hill and nearby suggest high status occupation in the Iron Age. By the seventh century it had become the centre of a royal estate, and for about 170 years after *c.* 665 a minster church occupied the hilltop, attached to an estate assessed at 50 hides, which was large enough to include land at Crowle 5 miles (8 km) to the south. By 836 this great estate

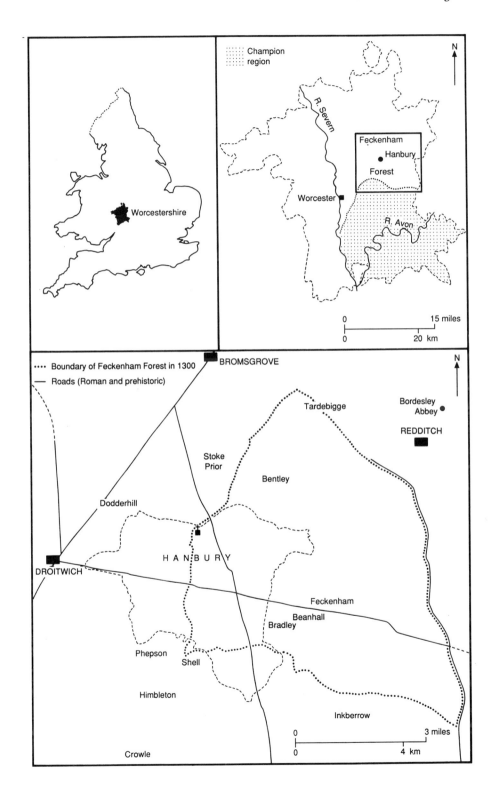

Champion region

R. Severn

Feckenham

Hanbury

Forest

Worcester

R. Avon

N

Worcestershire

0   15 miles

0   20 km

···· Boundary of Feckenham Forest in 1300
—— Roads (Roman and prehistoric)

BROMSGROVE

N

Tardebigge

Bordesley
Abbey

REDDITCH

Stoke
Prior

Bentley

Dodderhill

H A N B U R Y

DROITWICH

Feckenham

Beanhall
Bradley

Phepson

Shell

Himbleton

Inkberrow

Crowle

0   3 miles

0   4 km

was breaking up, but throughout the Middle Ages the manor of Hanbury remained a large and important one, capable of further dismemberment as more sub-manors were carved out of it, yet providing the bishops with substantial revenues. At some time between the ninth and eleventh centuries the houses of the group of clergy who had served the minster church were replaced by an establishment of the bishop's and accommodation for the parish priest; throughout the Middle Ages the manor house and the rectory shared the hilltop. Hanbury belonged to the bishopric estate of 17 manors (in 1086) rising to more than 20 in the thirteenth century. The lands of the estate were designed to straddle the whole of the diocese, extending from Bristol to north Warwickshire, partly to give the bishop a balance of resources from river valleys, the Cotswolds and the woodlands, and partly to provide him with a network of residences for his use on his circuits of the diocese. Perhaps bishops stayed at Hanbury in early times, but in the later Middle Ages they preferred Alvechurch with its gardens and park, and Hanbury became simply a source of revenue.[31]

The royal interest in Hanbury continued after it had been granted to the church. Feckenham immediately to the east, which was in the king's hands in the ninth century, served as the administrative centre of Feckenham Forest from the eleventh to the sixteenth century and as an important royal residence until the fourteenth (fig. 1). *Holeway* in the south-east of Hanbury parish was attached to Feckenham, until it was granted to Bordesley Abbey in about 1140 (fig. 2). After that date Feckenham Park, which stretched across the centre of Hanbury, remained a royal hunting preserve. The whole of Hanbury, and after 1300 its eastern half (fig. 1), lay within the royal forest, which meant that the inhabitants were liable to punishment in the forest courts if they damaged the vert (trees) or killed the venison.

This brief summary indicates the complexity of Hanbury's position within the medieval hierarchy of lordship and administration. Let us take as an example a peasant in the mid-thirteenth century, living at Broughton, a sub-manor of Hanbury (fig. 2), who would have paid rents to his lord, the Knights Templar, and attended their manor court. Twice each year he would have been summoned to the bishop of Worcester's view of frankpledge, which had jurisdiction over Hanbury and its sub-manors. He might also owe suit to the courts of the bishop's hundred of Oswaldslow. Our Broughton peasant worshipped in the church on Church Hill, and was subject to the ecclesiastical courts held by the rector.[32] The forest courts, both the lesser swanimotes and the occasional sessions of the justices of the forest could fine the Broughton peasant who offended against forest law. Like anyone else in the county, he could be involved in the proceedings of the royal courts when the justices sat at Worcester. As a tenant of the Templars, he might on occasion be summoned to the local preceptory of Temple Balsall in Warwickshire.

Such administrative arrangements were probably of secondary importance for people whose main preoccupation lay in the need to make a living from the land, and whose work was much influenced by the physical environment. Hanbury's relief (fig. 2), though relatively uneventful, includes some contrasts of high and low ground. In the north and east the land rises above the 100 m (300 ft) contour and Church Hill, Piper's Hill and Forest Hill are

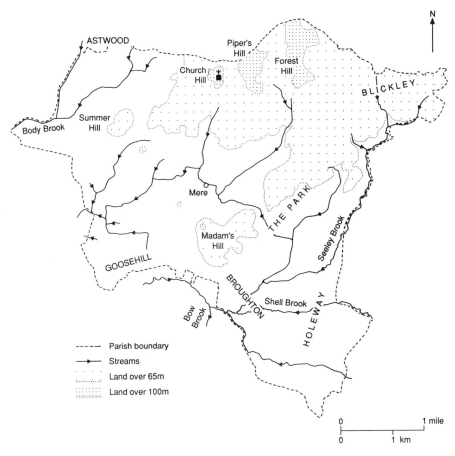

Figure 2   Topography of Hanbury parish: relief and drainage.

high enough to provide local landmarks. A spur runs south-west and rises to form a minor prominence at Madam's Hill. The ground falls away to the south and west, and the western parish boundary lies at 37–47 m (125–150 feet) above OD. Minor brooks and streams flow out of the hills towards the south and west. One system empties into the Body Brook which joins the River Salwarpe at Droitwich, and on the eastern side of the parish the Seeley Brook (called Berte Brook in the Middle Ages) joins with the Shell Brook (once known as Humel Brook) to run into the Bow Brook, a tributary of the Avon. The low-lying land in the south-west of the parish, where the largest medieval meadows lay, can be marshy in winter, and other pockets of boggy land can be found elsewhere, notably near the Mere in the centre of the parish.

The soils vary greatly from heavy clay to gravelly alluvium, but there are two main groups. In the whole of the north-west of the parish, north of the Goosehill meadows and west of a line drawn between Madam's Hill and Forest Hill, the soils belong to the Whimple 3 association.[33] The same association occurs in a broad band just to the north of the hamlet of Goosehill, in the south-west of the parish. The Whimple 3 association is dominated by reddish fine loamy or fine silty soils over clay, a drift component modifying the texture of the upper horizons of soils on Mercian mudstone (formerly known as Keuper Marl). On steeper slopes where drift is absent, the soils are clays. The soils are affected by slight seasonal waterlogging. They are regarded by modern farmers as fertile and quite easily cultivated, though they can be rather heavy and wet. They are classified by the modern Ministry of Agriculture as Grade 3 land, that is, of average quality, capable of being used either as arable or pasture.

The south and centre of the parish (the medieval districts of Goosehill, Broughton, *Holeway* and the Park), and the eastern extremity of Blickley have grey soils of three associations on similar geological substrata, Wickham 2, Evesham 2, and Denchworth. Wickham 2 association, for example, is dominated by fine loamy or clay soils on Jurassic clay shales. All three associations have similar characteristics. They now pose various problems for farmers because they tend to become waterlogged and are difficult to work in the spring. They are low in phosphorus. In consequence part of eastern Hanbury is classified by the Ministry as Grade 4 land, meaning that it suffers from sufficient limitations to make it best suited for pasture.

The modern assessment of these soils might lead us to suppose that the reddish Triassic soils would attract the earliest and most intensive cultivation, and the grey Jurassic clays would be more marginal, being used for cereal crops only when land-hunger motivated farmers. They would be left to revert to pasture and wood in times of retreat. To some extent, as will be seen, the medieval development of Hanbury accords with this prediction, but there are important local exceptions. If we take a broader view, in the West Midland region as a whole the grey clay soils of the Evesham 2 and Denchworth associations provided the environment for the nucleated villages and champion husbandry of the Warwickshire Feldon and parts of the Vale of Evesham, which are usually regarded as districts of early settlement and intensive cereal production. The Whimple 3 association in the north of the region is linked with woodland landscapes in the Middle Ages; they are traditionally described as areas of 'late' settlement. Generalizations about the 'natural' qualities of soils provide no easy answers to the problems of settlement history. Modern judgements are based on mechanized cultivation – soils on Jurassic clays are difficult to work in wet conditions with tractors. Perhaps Roman and medieval ploughs coped better with these conditions. Much depended then, and depends now, on the management of land. Modern farmers have certainly brushed aside the gloomy assessments of soil scientists, and cultivate as much land in south-east Hanbury on the sticky Denchworth association as do those farming on the red Triassic soils in the north-west of the parish.

In medieval and early modern times Hanbury belonged to the woodland landscape which stretched across the Midlands from south Shropshire to Staffordshire, north Worcestershire and north Warwickshire. These West Midland woodlands fitted the pattern described above, with their scattered hamlets, plentiful pasture and wood, enclosed and irregular fields, and free peasants. The woodlands can now be recognized by the modern visitor from their winding lanes, their old and often ragged hedges, containing many species of trees and bushes, and the small fields of irregular shape. Cottages have been squeezed into the roadside verges, or are sited away from the roads down dark tracks. Hanbury lies near the southern frontier of the Worcestershire woodland (fig. 1). The adjacent parish of Himbleton contains three hamlets in its northern section, but most of its inhabitants in the Middle Ages lived in a large nucleated village and worked open fields. To the south beyond Himbleton lies a succession of champion villages. Why should two neighbouring villages differ so markedly? Determinists might argue that the woodland inevitably resulted from the disadvantages of soils and climate, yet Hanbury is not untypical of the woodlands in that its soils were not especially intractable, nor its relief extreme, and its weather is not notably wet or cold.[34] It offered no special rewards to its cultivators, nor yet punished them with great obstacles to successful husbandry. We must take into account the human as well as the natural environment in weighing up the character of the woodlands. The inhabitants of Hanbury had the disadvantage of living under the regime of forest law, and many of them were tenants and subjects of a powerful and demanding lord, the bishop of Worcester. On the other hand, the woodlands offered resources that were often in short supply in the champion districts, such as pasture, timber and fuel. Hanbury's inhabitants also lived within the marketing zone of two towns, Bromsgrove and Droitwich, and the latter, which was the second largest town in Worcestershire, offered many opportunities for the sale of produce and for employment. Similar negative and positive influences must have been at work in earlier times, and it is to the periods before 1086 that we must now turn.

Chapter 2

Origins: Until Domesday

Until the 1970s very little evidence existed for prehistoric or Roman activity at Hanbury. We could well have believed the old assumption that the heavy soils and dense forests of the Midlands repelled early settlement. Our first consideration, then, must be to assess the extent of settlement in the area in the prehistoric, Roman and pre-Conquest periods, and then to attempt to explain its meaning in terms of economic and social structures.

PREHISTORY (fig. 3)

The evidence for the prehistoric period has come almost entirely from the systematic collection of artefacts from the plough soil in the programme of field-walking. This type of research poses many problems of method and interpretation. In an ideal world the field-walking would be conducted in identical controlled circumstances, so that the sample of material from one field could be compared with that from another. In practice conditions vary a good deal. The extent to which the soil has been broken down by cultivation, the degree of weathering, the direction and quantity of sunlight, the skill of the observer, will all lead to variations in the results. Some objects, such as flints and red Romano-British pottery, survive better in the soil and are more easily seen than poorly made pottery. There is also the problem of relating the surface finds to the below-ground remains. An isolated flint could have been a single specimen lost in antiquity by a traveller crossing an uninhabited waste; we tend to assume that it is representative of dozens more buried in layers of occupation debris. In general the results of field-walking will understate the extent of early occupation. Only a proportion of the land is available for investigation; discoveries will be made in pasture fields in the exceptional circumstances when the earth has been disturbed by animals or by the digging of trenches for pipes.

Hanbury contains dozens of fields of permanent pasture, which will appear as blank areas on any distribution map, yet may well contain as many sites as the arable. In ploughed fields the chief problem is that poor conditions will

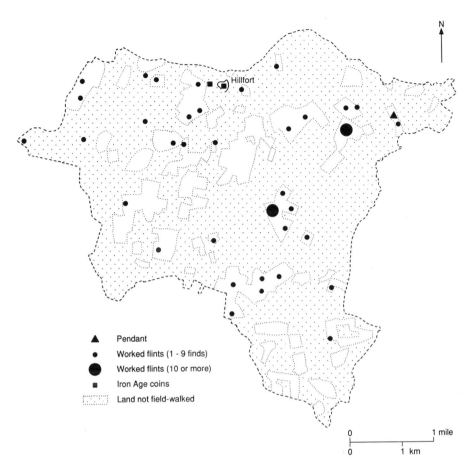

Figure 3 Prehistoric Hanbury.

prevent objects from appearing on the surface. If the layers containing flints, pottery and metalwork are deeply buried, they will not be touched by the plough; and if the soil has not been reduced to a fine tilth, or if the crop has begun to grow, objects will remain invisible. In view of these qualifications, the number of find-spots of objects, mainly flints, must reflect widespread prehistoric activity in Hanbury. In all, 38 sites have yielded material, mostly flakes (the by-product of flint-working), but also a number of small scrapers. These are not closely datable; one site has material of mesolithic type, but the majority seem to belong to the Neolithic or Bronze Age.[1] One out-of-the-ordinary object from Ditchford Bank is a small green-stone pendant, shaped like a whetstone but probably used as an ornament, which is paralleled by finds in Bronze Age barrows.[2] Five sites have produced fragments of pebbles, which have been cracked and split by burning and rapid cooling. Single examples cannot be dated, and so the find-spots have not been included on the map. Some may well have come from mounds of such stones, found in stream banks elsewhere in the West Midlands, which are dated by radiocarbon methods to the Bronze Age, or from prehistoric settlement sites.[3]

Isolated finds of flints and other objects could be attributed to the losses of itinerant parties hunting in woods and wastes. The amount of material, however, must show that Hanbury was permanently settled by people practising agriculture. This would accord with scientific evidence from river banks of widespread clearance of trees in the West Midlands in the Bronze Age, which led to the deposition of water-borne silts originating as run-off from cultivated fields.[4] Hanbury's prehistoric finds occur on all types of soil and are found in a wide range of places, both close to streams (eleven sites) and on high ground (six sites), and in every other situation between these extremes. Two of the largest concentrations of flints lie on hilltop sites. The only part of the parish where they seem to be absent is in the south-eastern corner, so perhaps some land there remained unsettled.

Flints have been found on sites which have also produced material of later periods. In six cases they are associated with concentrations of Romano-British pottery, but there is little to suggest a strong coincidence of sites from one period to another. No doubt more continuity between prehistoric and Roman settlement would be apparent if we had more information about the Iron Age. Unfortunately the pottery of this period does not seem to survive in the plough soil, and only a single possible Iron Age sherd has been found.[5] There are, however, good reasons to suppose settlement in association with the hill-fort on Church Hill. This fort only came to be recognized by prehistorians in the 1970s, though the circuit of fortifications is clearly marked on all sides, in an eroded state on the east and more prominently in the west. Its entrance lay in the south-west, where a holloway leads through the ramparts. Inside the fort a Dobunnic coin was found in the last century, and more recently two others have been reported from a field immediately to the west, and a fourth a kilometre to the north in Dodderhill parish.[6] Hill-forts are unlikely to have existed in isolation. In addition to the clear ground that must have existed in the immediate vicinity of the ramparts for reasons of military security, the builders must have drawn on a much larger area for labour to construct and maintain the banks, ditches and palisades, and if the hill-top was inhabited, food and tribute were no doubt gathered from the small farms of the neighbourhood. In other words, a hill-fort is the now visible apex of a once complex hierarchy of settlements. Possible traces of agricultural activity at this time are the substantial lynchets created by early ploughing, some of which seem to predate the ridge and furrow, but such features cannot be assigned to any specific period.[7]

A further piece of indirect evidence accords with the view that Hanbury supported a considerable Iron Age population. The salt industry of Droitwich is known to have been in operation from the second century BC.[8] The needs of the industry for fuel, presumably produced in managed coppices, and of the workers for food, must have led to the development of Droitwich's hinterland, and settlements in western Hanbury at least must have been influenced by this demand.

THE ROMANO-BRITISH PERIOD (fig. 4)

The abundance of Romano-British evidence allows us to make a fuller and less speculative reconstruction of Hanbury's settlement pattern between the first and fourth centuries AD. Two long-distance roads ran through the area studied, one from west to east linking Droitwich with Alcester, and ultimately leading into north Oxfordshire, and a north–south road from Bromsgrove that crossed the Avon near Fladbury and led on to the Cotswolds. The former was built no doubt in the first century as a military road, but later in its existence served to transport salt. The latter route, which is not as straight as the west–east road, and bypasses Droitwich, might have pre-Roman origins. Both roads coincide with modern roads for part of their length, but must be traced along footpaths and hedge-lines in the south and east of the parish. These important roads would have linked with a network of minor tracks which served the numerous local settlements. Remnants of them may still survive in the modern road system of the parish, such as the lanes converging on Church Hill.

Romano-British material has been recovered from 103 find-spots in

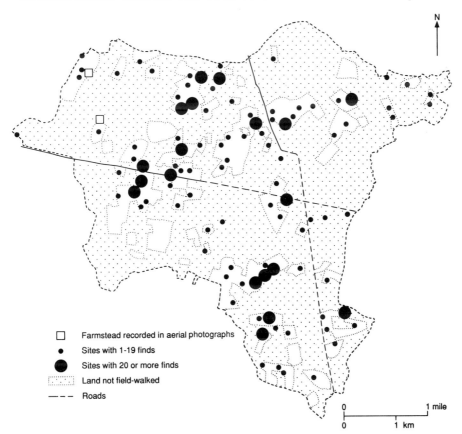

	Farmstead recorded in aerial photographs
•	Sites with 1-19 finds
●	Sites with 20 or more finds
	Land not field-walked
– – –	Roads

Figure 4   Romano-British Hanbury.

Hanbury (fig. 4). The majority of these consist of thin scatters of pottery, often at a density no higher than five sherds from a 10-acre (4 ha) field. This is taken to show that the land was cultivated in the Roman period, and that the pottery, having been thrown onto a midden along with domestic rubbish and farm muck, was then spread on the land in the process of manuring. Thin scatters may however sometimes occur in fields containing settlement sites. In the north-west corner of Hanbury, at Astwood, a field where only a few sherds have been found appears in an aerial photograph to contain a rectangular ditched enclosure, which is normally taken to mark the site of an Iron Age or Romano-British farmstead.[9] The material of the Roman period probably lies below the level to which the plough normally penetrates. This reminds us again that field-walking gives us a minimum of evidence – the rash of spots on the distribution map in no way exaggerates the extent of settlement of Hanbury in the Roman period.

Greater concentrations of Roman finds, defined arbitrarily in the case of field-walking as sites producing more than 20 sherds of pottery, occur in 19 places. These ought to indicate the sites of settlements or at least the proximity of these fields to Roman occupation. The character of the settlements is indicated by air photographs showing two farmsteads on the western edge of the parish, which resemble many others from the West Midlands region.[10] They consist of ditches enclosing a small rectangle (1.25 acres or 0.5 ha in area at most) in which stood timber buildings. The farmsteads are associated with the ditches of field systems. Where there is no evidence from air photographs, many of the denser pottery scatters are concentrated in a small space no more than 150 yards across, suggesting again the presence of small isolated farms. Durable building materials, such as stone, tile, or *tesserae* from floors, have not been found, so the buildings were presumably of timber, wattle and daub.

The finds do not suggest a very high level of material culture, as the locally made coarse pottery, Severn Valley ware, predominates overwhelmingly, accounting for 88 per cent to 98 per cent of the sherds from different sites.[11] Evidently imported pottery like Samian ware, or specialist wares made within Britain such as black-burnished ware or *mortaria*, all of which would have been readily obtainable at nearby Droitwich, were beyond the reach of Hanbury's inhabitants in any quantity. They were engaged in primary agricultural production, providing for their own needs of food, and having a limited surplus to exchange for manufactured goods. It might be thought that field-walking produces a biased sample of pottery, and if sites were excavated they might yield different results. However, the pottery dug from a Romano-British rubbish-pit found in preparing a site for a barn at Howning's Farm tells much the same story as the surface finds. The number of sherds of black-burnished ware (52) may seem impressive, and there were 9 pieces of Samian ware, but pottery from the site was very abundant, 753 sherds in all, and 84 per cent of the total consisted of the monotonous red and buff Severn Valley ware. Indeed the Samian came mainly from a single dish (type 18/31) which showed signs of heavy wear, as if it had been kept as a precious heirloom for a very long time; one piece bore the marks of a rivet, showing that its period of use had been prolonged with a repair.

Metalwork and coins suggestive of higher status settlements occur on a few sites, notably one just to the south of the Roman road, where coins have been found together with a brooch and a bronze figure of a lion, which originally formed part of a group of statuettes representing the goddess Cybele.[12] A bronze 'dolphin' brooch of about AD 100 has been found in eastern Hanbury in the valley of the Seeley Brook.[13] Perhaps the best candidate for a site of importance is Church Hill, which may have retained some significance after the hill-fort ceased to be a military strong point. Certainly many coins have been found on and near the hill, and by analogy with other hill-forts that were occupied in the Roman period, the site may have been used for religious purposes.[14]

In making a general assessment of the state of Hanbury in Roman times our first impression must be of the widespread nature of settlement. We cannot avoid the conclusion that cultivation extended over virtually the whole area; the gaps can be explained usually by the modern use of the land for pasture, which makes field-walking impossible. A real absence of evidence is apparent in the Goosehill area in the south-west, where many fields have been walked but no Romano-British pottery found, and it is likely that this low-lying ground was used in Roman times, as in the Middle Ages, mainly as meadow and wood. Otherwise Roman material is found everywhere, on all types of soil and terrain, including land which was wooded in the Middle Ages. The Roman period lasted for four centuries, and it would be dangerous to assume that all of our sites were in simultaneous occupation. In fact, the best dating evidence from two sites which have produced coins shows a wide range from the first to the third century (on Church Hill) and from the first to the fourth (south of the Roman road). The pottery from Hownings Farm dates from the second, third and fourth centuries. So these three sites at least had an extended life covering most of the period.

There are two ways of estimating the overall scale of the Roman settlement of Hanbury. One is to extrapolate from the known sites to make allowance for the undiscovered and undiscoverable ones. It might be alleged that the sample is biased, because modern farmers choose the best land for cultivation, and so did the Romano-British peasants; therefore the modern arable contains most of the early settlements, and the modern pasture fields were once wastes. This is unlikely as farmers now seem to select fields for ploughing for a wide range of reasons, of which soil quality is only one. During the Hanbury survey fields of permanent pasture were ploughed up or disturbed in other ways, and these yielded their fair share of Romano-British pottery. So if as many Roman sites lie undiscovered in the two-thirds of the parish that cannot be field-walked, as are known in the one-third that has been investigated, a conservative total for the period can be calculated at 60 settlements. The other method of estimation is to compare the quantity of Roman pottery with that from the period 1100–1500. We know from documentary sources that in the later period the number of households fluctuated between 60 and 160. As the Roman finds are more abundant, there could have been at least as many households between the first and fourth centuries. There are problems in accepting this line of reasoning, as many medieval sites lie hidden beneath modern houses, and in any case

Roman pottery may have been manufactured in such quantities and so cheaply that each peasant household owned and broke more vessels than did their medieval successors. Clearly we cannot arrive at any dogmatic figure, but it would be reasonable to expect the level of the Romano-British population to have been of similar size to that of the Middle Ages.[15]

The Romano-British settlements consisted mainly of isolated farmsteads, though grouping of sites is apparent around the Roman road towards the west and in the Broughton area in the south. There is no hint of closely nucleated settlements; it is quite possible that some may belong to lines of farmsteads of the 'ladder' or 'girdle' type which have been recognized in other parts of Britain.[16] The absence of evidence of structural sophistication rules out identifying any of our sites as a 'villa'; indeed, with the exception of the rather special case of the Bays Meadow site at Droitwich, none has been found in north Worcestershire. A likely explanation is that like the Fenland or Cranborne Chase, Hanbury lay in an imperial estate, perhaps centred on Droitwich, where the salt supplies would have been exploited as an industry under the control of the state.[17] Another possibility is that Hanbury lay within a smaller territory dependent on Droitwich. Setting aside speculations about the government of the area, we may presume, as at other periods, that the economic presence of the town helped to stimulate production in the surrounding countryside. Hanbury's inhabitants would have been burdened with the taxes imposed by the Roman imperial government, and this drain on their resources no doubt contributed to their relatively poor material culture. On the other hand, they enjoyed some of the benefits of the stability and order of the imperial system, including access to the trading network where they could sell produce and buy manufactured goods. The numerous settlements and the extensive cultivation reflect the economic expansion of the period, and appreciation of this achievement heightens our sense of a collapse after the fourth century. Was the disappearance of industry, trade and the use of money accompanied by a crisis in the peasant economy also? It is sometimes alleged that peasants could have continued to produce for their own subsistence, but can we believe that a whole economic system with a substantial marketing sector could suffer such a crisis without repercussions at the level of the peasant producers?[18] Some of them, for example, may have been growing cash crops for distant markets. One thinks of the flax recorded in later periods in Hanbury's history; or the ale-brewing or dairying implied by the tankards and strainers made of Severn Valley ware. The reduction in demand for commodities such as these must have created difficulties for the primary producers. But in the absence of concrete evidence, which can only come from a programme of excavation, these thoughts are bound to be hypothetical. The field-work that has been done allows us to make one clear generalization: that many of the Romano-British settlement sites were abandoned, not necessarily immediately after 400, but none the less totally deserted. In the Middle Ages their sites were used as arable land, as pasture or as wood. In only five cases do concentrations of Roman finds coincide with medieval settlements, and one of those was the important but exceptional case of Church Hill. Between the end of the Roman period and the high Middle Ages the settlement pattern was transformed.

400–1086

If we relied on archaeological evidence alone, we should be forced to conclude that Hanbury was largely uninhabited between 400 and 1100. In theory material of the period ought to be available for recovery from the fields, because pagan Saxon and middle Saxon pottery is known from sites in the Avon valley, and by the tenth and eleventh centuries well-made wares were in use in the towns of Worcester and Droitwich.[19] However, such pottery seems to be associated with high-status places, and it is typical of such finds that the only piece from Hanbury that could be of middle Saxon date was found in the churchyard on Church Hill. However, the existence of peasant settlements at Hanbury to complement the important hill-top site cannot be doubted.

The earliest Hanbury document has been lost, but notes were made of its contents in the seventeenth century when it was still preserved at Worcester.[20] It was a charter of the Mercian ruler Wulfhere (657–74) by which the king granted a 50-hide estate at *Heanburg* to Abbot Colman (an Irish name) with rights of inheritance. We ought to be suspicious of a document claiming to have been issued at such an early date, and must wonder why it was not copied into one of the eleventh-century Worcester cartularies.[21] On the other hand we ought not to dismiss it on the grounds of its date, and it is possible that as it made no grant to Worcester, the Worcester monks would not have felt the need to include it in cartularies, whose function was to defend their interests. One cannot imagine what advantage would be gained by a forger from its fabrication.

If we treat the Hanbury 'charter' as genuine, it gives us some useful information: that the place had gained its English name, meaning the 'high fortification', which in turn demonstrates the continued importance of the hill-fort on Church Hill. It was presumably there that Colman built his monastery, or minster church. While the 50-hide estate may have been created at the time of the charter, Wulfhere was probably granting intact an existing royal estate, part of the large section of north-east Worcestershire that had been held by the kings of Mercia. The reference in the charter to brine-pits has already been mentioned as evidence of Hanbury's long-term connection with Droitwich salt-making. The '50 hides' implies the existence on the estate of people and settlements as well as land, because such assessments depended on productive capacity, in other words, human as well as material resources.

The seventh-century estate must have extended far beyond the later parish of Hanbury, which was rated at 14 hides in the eleventh century. A charter of 836, which survives in its original form, and is undoubtedly authentic, records the dismembering of the Hanbury estate.[22] It belongs to a group of Mercian charters of the period, which in contrast to the generous gifts to the church in the previous century, show the kings of Mercia selling or bartering privileges to the church.[23] In this case the Hanbury minster gained various exemptions from obligations such as feeding the king and his servants, in return for surrenders of 50 hides to the king and an *ealdorman*. Four sections of the estate are named in the charter itself, and four in later annotations (fig. 1). From this we can deduce that the Hanbury estate consisted of a piece of land called Hanbury or alternatively *Haeccaham*; another called *Felda* or *beansetum*, which is thought to refer to Beanhall in the western part of Feckenham; Crowle which lies 5 miles (8 km) to the south; and a place called 'Idsall'. 'Idsall' is close to an early form of the name of Shifnal in Shropshire, and it has been suggested that this records a long-distance attachment of lands of the kind that is well known in Kent or Warwickshire.[24] Perhaps the association of a place called *Heanbyrig* with Shifnal in lists of lands of Peterborough Abbey strengthened this view.[25] However, it seems unlikely that the Peterborough property is our Hanbury. Usually places with dissimilar resources, such as arable and woodland, were connected in this way, but Hanbury's and Shifnal's landscapes probably resembled one another. Another possibility is that Idsall was an old name for part of Himbleton, the parish which lies to the south of Hanbury, and which, like Hanbury, Feckenham and Crowle, belonged to the hundred of Esch in the eleventh century. According to Domesday, Crowle was a detached berewick of Phepson, which lies in north Himbleton, and in the later Middle Ages the chapelry of Shell (another Himbleton hamlet), was dependent on Hanbury church.[26] It must seem surprising that the original Hanbury estate should not have extended to the north, as Church Hill stands so near to the northern boundary of the parish. However, all of the evidence suggests that Dodderhill and Stoke Prior belonged to different estate complexes, and that the Hanbury estate lay to the south and east of the monastery on Church Hill.

All of this tells us only a little about Hanbury itself, except that the minster church was diminishing in importance in the ninth century, not just because it gave up much of its endowment, but also, as the charter makes plain, because the bishop of Worcester was playing an important role in the monastery's affairs. He gave a large sum of money to an *ealdorman* as part of the complex compromise of 836, and the Hanbury lands, after the king and his followers had enjoyed them for the remainder of their lives, were to revert to the church of Worcester. If he had not done so already, the bishop would become the lord of the minster's lands, in accordance with a pattern of aggrandizement that was pursued by successive bishops of Worcester, and by contemporary prelates, such as the archbishops of Canterbury.[27] Presumably for the first century or two of its existence the minster was served by a group of clergy, who lived with their servants and even their wives in the protection of the hillfort. Their numbers decreased later, until by 1086 only one priest is recorded.

The minster's estate was worth coveting because it included a substantial share in the Droitwich salt industry, and because it contained landed resources inhabited by peasants, whose settlements are called in the conventional formulae of the 836 charter 'small houses' (*casallis*). We must assume that throughout the period, in spite of the economic and political upheavals of the transition from the Roman Empire to the English kingdoms, people continued to occupy at least the western part of Hanbury. One place in the north-west near Astwood was called Walmer, 'the pool of the Welsh'.[28] British people must have been living there, conceivably still in the farmstead surrounded by a ditch known from aerial photographs, but when the name was coined, perhaps in the seventh or eighth century, another section of the local population were speaking Old English, and regarded the British as foreign. We cannot know if there had been a large incursion of Anglo-Saxon migrants, or whether people of British origin changed their language to English and identified themselves with the dominant newcomers. Pagan cemeteries with grave goods of Germanic type occur in the West Midlands, in the Avon valley and as far north in Worcestershire as Upton Snodsbury, 6 miles (10 km) to the south of Hanbury, but are absent from the north and west of the county. This could be taken to mean that no Anglo-Saxon penetrated into the area in the sixth and seventh centuries, but this is unlikely because of the prevalence of English place-names. Perhaps there were migrants, but they were converted to Christianity by the priests of the British church, and so were buried in a Christian fashion without grave goods, leaving no distinctive archaeological traces in consequence. It still seems implausible that mass-migration took place, but rather that a powerful and influential minority were able to persuade the native population to speak the language of the new élite.

Again the Droitwich link helps our understanding of Hanbury's history. Fifth-century evidence has come from Bays Meadow, and at the Upwich salt-pit hearths were working in the fifth and sixth centuries; documents in the seventh and eighth centuries refer to Droitwich's salt-making.[29] Production of such a basic commodity is likely to have continued throughout the whole period. Rural settlements nearby would have had some connection with the industry, if only as a source of labour. At least part of the road system survived in this period, not just the salt-way running eastward from Droitwich, but also the north-south road, which gave *Holeway* (holloway) its name.[30]

The breakup of the Hanbury estate in the ninth century left the bishops of Worcester in effective control of most of the area covered by the later parish. There are indications that the estate was only patchily and not very intensively settled. In the tenth and early eleventh century the bishops felt the need to issue leases of land for the benefit of layman, mostly called *cniht* or *thegn*, in a pattern of land tenure that resembles later feudalism. They generally detached pieces of land assessed at between one and 6 hides to make these grants. So at Fladbury in the Avon valley, once an estate of 44 hides, the bishop retained the best land near the river as his demesne manor, but granted out the northern parts, such as Ab Lench and Hill and Moor.[31] Little of Hanbury was alienated in this way after the ninth-century dismemberment, most probably because its outlying territories, the places that had already gained names such as Blickley and Broughton, had not developed sufficiently to provide a *thegn* with an adequate living. Some fragmentation of the estate is first recorded in Domesday: a very small manor had been granted to a tenant at Astwood. The place-name means 'eastern wood', and also occurs in adjacent Dodderhill parish, suggesting that a large wood in pre-Conquest times straddled the boundary.[32] It was probably named in relation to Droitwich, which also had a Westwood. The wood name could mean that this new manor was formed out of cleared land. At the time of Domesday, the king held *Holeway*, by some arrangement of unknown origin, which could well go back to the ninth century. He had also established the Park which stretched across the centre of the parish, and became a major intrusion on the landscape, forcing the diversion of both of the main roads.

In 1086, large areas of the parish lay under grass and trees in the royal Park, which together with the wood belonging to the manor of *Holeway* could have accounted for more than a thousand acres. The bishop's woods contained between 500 and 700 acres, using the customary formula to convert 'one league by half a league' (fig. 5).[33] The cultivated area can be estimated at between 1,000 and 2,000 acres, with 2 demesne ploughs in the bishop's manor, 3 at *Holeway*, and a combined total of 27 tenant ploughs.[34] Even 2,000 acres would fill only a quarter of the parish. Perhaps in this case the 'two hides of waste' mentioned in Domesday really refers to unoccupied land, and is not the administrative device that has been shown to lie behind the term in other Domesday entries.[35] The population looks decidedly thin, with only 34 peasants at Hanbury and 5 at *Holeway*, who together with the reeve and priest at the former manor and the reeve and beadle at *Holeway* make a total of only 43 households. Even if we count Hanbury's 5 slaves and *Holeway's* 6 as potential peasant households, we still have less than 60 households stretched over 12 square miles, making a density of 22 people per square mile (9 per sq km), which is near to the low average prevailing in north Worcestershire.[36] Domesday may have omitted some people. In the twelfth century a *radman* is known to have lived in Hanbury: he was a tenant of high standing, who performed administrative and escort services. *Radmen* originated in the pre-Conquest period, and it is very likely, unless the Domesday reeve is equated with the *radman*, that the 1086 survey missed out this important household. Domesday tells us that at Astwood the sub-tenant Ralph 'has 1 plough'; this implement cannot have been worked without labour, and either tenants or slaves must have lived on that small manor.

Even taking into account Domesday's undercounting of people, it still seems likely that the people and fields of eleventh-century Hanbury were concentrated in two restricted areas of the parish, in the north-west and south-east (zone A in fig. 5). This identification of the area of Domesday settlement is based on backward reading from later topographical evidence, which will be briefly indicated here but discussed in more detail below. Evidence for new settlements in the twelfth and thirteenth centuries, both new manors and peasant assarts, is concentrated in the eastern part of the parish, along the edge of the Park and at Blickley, and in the south-west at Goosehill and Broughton. The place-name Blickley (Blica's *leah* or clearing) shows that some use was made of the eastern end of Hanbury before the twelfth century, but one suspects on a small scale. This leaves the land to the west of the church and north of Goosehill as the most intensely settled. Within that area were concentrated various elements in the landscape which are likely to be of early origin: the core of the bishop's demesne, most of the holdings of the customary tenants, and the open-field arable. *Holeway* is less well documented, but its boundaries are known, so we can say with confidence that its inhabitants were confined to the south-eastern corner of the parish (fig. 6).[37]

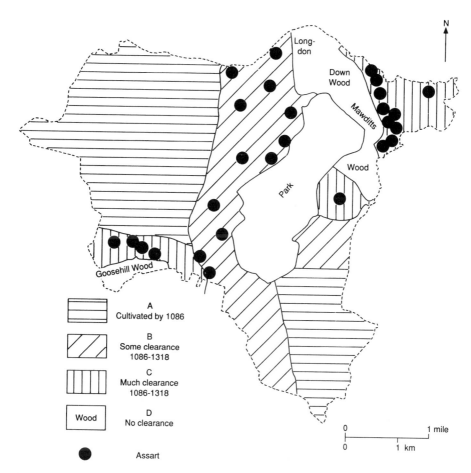

Figure 5   Settlement zones in Hanbury, 400-1318.

We cannot be sure for how long these two large enclaves of settlements and cultivation had been functioning before Domesday. There is every likelihood that part of these developed lands had in fact been farmed since the Roman period. However, this element of continuity should not lead us to underrate the great transformation in the use of land that had overtaken the whole of central and north-eastern Hanbury. In the king's Park 'wild animals' (ferae) roamed where once Romano-British farmers had tilled the soil. In the north-eastern extremity of Hanbury a Bronze Age farmer had worn, and lost, his ornamental pendant, and a prosperous Romano-British peasant's wife her dolphin brooch, but by the eleventh century woods and grassland stretched towards Bradley and Feckenham. We do not know whether this retreat of settlement and expansion of wood and pasture was simply the result of a shrinkage of population or an act of policy. The designation of a large area as a royal park might suggest at least an element of decision-making by higher authority, though of course the king's officials may have chosen already depopulated land for the Park. Nor do we know when these great changes took place. The old presumption that a cataclysm overtook the population of the Roman province soon after 410 is known to be an oversimplification. The changes in land use may have occurred much later. No doubt when we compare the evidence for a stretch of countryside in late Roman times and the eleventh century we should expect to find as many and complex a series of changes in the intervening period as those which occurred in the better-documented seven centuries that followed 1086.

Finally, we must ask how Hanbury's inhabitants were organized by their rulers and lords in the pre-Conquest centuries. The 50-hide estate of the seventh and eighth centuries supplied tribute and services to both the clergy of the minster and the king, and perhaps the bishops too. The clauses of exemption in the charter of 836 reveal the obligations to the king as assistance in the building of his residences (perhaps at Droitwich or Bromsgrove), and provision of food for the king himself, his *ealdormen* and his messengers. The clergy in the minster church would likewise have demanded occasional labour services, and food rents, like the ale, mead, cows, sheep, hams, cheese and bread which were delivered to the Worcester clergy each year from an estate at Kempsey, according to a mid-ninth-century document.[38] The estate was probably divided at an early stage into the sections named in 836, so the food rents could have been allocated among the different parts: we could guess that each year Beanhall provided food for ten weeks, Crowle for ten weeks and so on, depending on the capacity of the land. The exploitation of such large units of land elsewhere was co-ordinated by ministerial tenants, that is, administrators granted holdings.[39] Such a figure, a *radman*, as has been mentioned, survived at Hanbury in the twelfth century, at Wybbe's holding located near Church Hill, and there may have been one or two more who appear as well-endowed freeholdings in the survey of *c.*1170. Large estates like the 50 hides at Hanbury were expected to provide revenues for more than one dominant household, but in view of the indications of the size of the food rents and the quantities of service required from similar estates, we must conjecture that the demands were not especially oppressive.[40] The obligations were spread out over a great deal of land and dozens of peasants, and the heaviest tasks would have been performed by slaves, whose existence was taken for granted by contemporaries but must not be forgotten by us.

The system of tribute collection, having some resemblance to the tax-gathering of the late Roman Empire, changed radically in the ninth century. The breakdown of the 50 hides probably began before 836, but the division of that year represents an important stage in the separation of Hanbury itself from the outliers at Crowle, Beanhall and Himbleton. With the dis-memberment of the estate, the clergy of the minster and ultimately the bishop had to adapt themselves to extracting their livelihood from a much smaller area of land. Now the demesne increased in significance. Presumably the minster already used an area of land as a 'home farm', which may well, like the core of the medieval demesne, have been located near to Church Hill. By the time of Domesday it was cultivated by two ploughs worked by four male slaves. The single female slave could have looked after the bishop's herd of cows. Any other tasks on the demesne, including harvesting and haymaking, depended on the labour services of the 16 *villani*, and to a lesser extent on the 18 bordars. The latter, whose smallholdings would have left them with spare time to work for others, could have been hired to serve the demesne both for full-time tasks such as shepherding, and for more casual labour at time of peak demand, notably the harvest. In the eleventh century the two elements of the manor's organization, the demesne and the tenant lands, were complementary resources providing the lords of Hanbury with their revenues. By the twelfth century the Hanbury peasants were heavily burdened with agricultural services, the inevitable result of the system of management that was probably introduced in the ninth century.[41] Tribute survived in the twelfth century in the vestigial form of a rent paid in salt, which must belong to the time when the Hanbury peasants themselves worked at boiling the brine at Droitwich.

The 50-hide estate, and its smaller successors in the ninth century, depended primarily on renders in kind or in labour, reflecting the small importance of the market in the rural economy, which in turn prevented much payment of rents in cash. By 1066 Hanbury manor was valued at £7, which represents not an actual annual revenue, but the potential if the manor was let at farm. At that stage, like the *gebur* in the eleventh-century treatise on the obligations of West Midland peasants, the Hanbury tenants could have been paying as part of their obligations at least 10d a year, and probably much more.[42] There may even have been tenants paying cash rents only who were omitted from the Domesday survey.[43] The manor had a very direct relationship with the urban economy, because it received annually 105 mitts (840 bushels) of salt from Droitwich. Together with the 220 mitts belonging to two other bishopric manors, this gave the whole Worcester estate plenty of salt for its internal needs and a saleable surplus. The other manor in the parish recorded in Domesday, *Holeway*, had connections with Worcester where it once had three houses but retained only one. These could have been used to sell produce and purchase goods for the manor, like the two ploughshares that the Worcester houses paid as a rent in 1086. Before the urbanization of the period 850–1050, the revenues from rural estates were limited by the difficulties of storing and using foodstuffs and other consumable goods. There was no point in heaping up vast stocks of grain and meat beyond the amounts necessary to feed a household. As the market expanded and the urban population grew, lords were given the incentive to step up both demesne production and their demands on peasants, in the knowledge that surpluses could be exchanged for cash or other goods.[44]

All of this can be seen functioning within the agrarian landscape of the eleventh century. The demesne arable and the tenant holdings were concentrated in north-west Hanbury, and at *Holeway* in the south-east. Here much grain was produced both for subsistence and for exchange. The abundant grassland and wood was partly reserved for the pleasures of the king, and the bishop also, judging from the statement in Domesday that the woods of Bradley, which may well have included parts of Blickley in east Hanbury, gave 'the proceeds in hunting' to the manor of Fladbury.[45] Above all the grazing must have yielded useful surpluses of milk and meat for sale, and the woods were managed to provide fuel for the Droitwich salt-pans, probably a hundred cartloads of wood each year for the 105 mitts of salt.[46]

Chapter 3

Hanbury in its Prime: Eleventh to Fourteenth Century

THE GREAT EXPANSION, 1086–1318

Historians have long believed that rural society in all its aspects, but in particular the amount of land under cultivation, greatly expanded in the twelfth and thirteenth centuries. Some see this as the tail-end of long-term growth that had been in full swing for two or three centuries before 1000, and others as a new movement.[1] Doubt has been cast on the whole concept of growth by the advocates of continuity, who believe that, as the whole landscape had been utilized since prehistoric times, there was surely little scope for more than a modest extension of cultivation at such a late date.[2]

We can give only complex answers to such simple questions. Much depends on the region examined. In, say, the champion or feldon districts of the West Midlands, the continuity theory has much to commend it, as there is little evidence for clearance of new land at any time in the last two millennia. The story in the woodlands is different, but by no means uniformly so. At Hanbury the north-west and south-east sections of the parish (zone A in fig. 5), perhaps a third of the total, were occupied continuously over a long period, possibly since prehistoric times. In other parts of the parish discontinuity prevailed. After virtually the whole area had been farmed in the Roman period, much woodland regenerated, to the point that the expansion of the early Middle Ages involved little clearance of primeval wild wood. Rather the assarters must often have encountered in their work the eroded and overgrown banks and ditches of Romano-British farmsteads and field systems: they were recolonizing abandoned land.[3]

Reclamation of wood and waste proceeded on a small scale in the twelfth century, and more rapidly in the thirteenth. Table 1 estimates the increase in population from 1086 to 1299, showing that after a first century of modest growth, numbers doubled between *c.* 1170 and 1299.[4]

This was not an especially remarkable increase. In the country as a whole the population is thought to have tripled between 1086 and 1300, and many woodland manors show a four or fivefold rise in numbers of tenants.[5] Perhaps the calculation is inaccurate, because the population of the smaller

Table 1.   The population of Hanbury, 1086–1299

Date	Hanbury manor	Holeway manor	Broughton manor (with Becknor)	Others	Total	Multiplier	TOTAL
1086	41*	13*	(in Hanbury)	5§	59	4.5	266
c. 1170	45	15	10	10	80	4.5	360
1299	91	30†	20	20	161	4.5	725

(households in the first five columns, individuals in the last column)

Notes

* counting slaves, and (at Hanbury) a priest as the heads of households.
§ including the tenant of the sub-manor of Astwood, with an estimate of 3 for his tenants, and the *radman*. Another 5 or 10 households could well have been omitted from Domesday.
† including an estimate for *Knottenhull*.

manors is based largely on guesswork and there are problems in estimating the number of subtenants. However, the figures reflect the fact that expansion was inhibited at Hanbury by the deliberate conservation of woods and pastures by the king, the bishop and other lords. We normally think that forest law did not prevent the colonizers' work: it merely regulated clearance, and assarts were allowed providing that the king received payments of money.[6] In this case, however, the physical barrier of the pale around the royal Park, and the special protection that the Park was given, kept the assarts at bay. Only in the south-west corner does the Park boundary seem to carry the marks of encroachments. For the bishops' and other private woods, the chief obstacle to clearance lay in the desire of the lords to maintain their valuable assets in such close proximity to the fuel-hungry salt-houses of Droitwich. In any case, at times in the twelfth century there was some fall in the demand for land, and three yardlands lay vacant in *c.* 1170.[7]

The proliferation of small manors had some connection with agricultural expansion. The usual pattern was to create new manors only when sufficient peasants were available to provide them with rents and labour, though new lords, anxious to increase their revenues, no doubt promoted settlement and the extension of cultivation. As we have seen, before 1086 only Astwood and the modest holding of the *radman*, both in the north-west of the parish, seem to have been detached from the main manor of Hanbury (fig. 6). In the early twelfth century a large piece of land at Broughton, assessed at about 6 hides, was granted to a branch of the Beauchamp family.[8] In the early 1220s it passed into the hands of the order of the Knights Templar, and has ever since been called Temple Broughton.[9] Later in the twelfth century *Becknor* manor was carved out of land to the north of Broughton, and at the same time we become aware of a holding in the centre of the north-western zone, in the hands of the de Hanbury family, which was later known as Hamburys.[10] These last two holdings, like Astwood, were rated at only a half-hide. On the eastern side of the parish the royal manor of *Holeway* had come into the hands of the Cistercian monks of Bordesley in about 1140; it became a monastic grange, and spawned a second grange to the north at *Knottenhull* in the early thirteenth century.[11] At some time a secular manor was established between the two granges for the hereditary keepers of the royal Park, later known as Park Hall.[12] Blickley in the north-east was not granted out to feudal tenants, but was kept by the bishops as a detached part of Hanbury. As it developed its own demesne and the tenants increased in number the bishops built a *curia* (farmyard) there, and in the late thirteenth century Blickley was being described as a separate manor.[13]

Therefore by 1240 centrifugal forces at Hanbury had created no less than eight separate sub-manors or units of land management: the royal Park, the four lay manors of Astwood, *Becknor*, Hamburys and Park Hall, and three church properties at Temple Broughton, *Holeway* and *Knottenhull*. Shortly afterwards Blickley was emerging as a ninth subdivision. Wybbes might rate as a tenth (fig. 6). Of these the Park was uninhabited, and *Knottenhull* may well have housed no more than the lay brothers and servants of Bordesley Abbey. The others were more conventional manors, and peasant rents and labour contributed to their value – £6 3s. 0d. being *Holeway's* assessment in the twelfth century, while Broughton was judged to be worth £4 when it lay in the king's hands after its confiscation from Walter Beauchamp in 1170.[12] In 1086 Hanbury had been a manor providing the bishop of Worcester with just 2.2 per cent of the value of his estates, and *Holeway* contributed a much smaller fraction of the revenues of the king. Two centuries later, of the eight manors, the largest gave the bishop 3.3 per cent of his income, two helped to defray the costs of religious houses (Bordesley and the Balsall preceptory of the Templars), and the rest furnished all or a large part of the livelihood of five gentry families.[15]

Expansion had been achieved by increasing the intensity of the use of existing resources and by the clearance of new land. The former process can be seen at work in the late twelfth century on the bishop's manor when a dozen yardlands (one yardland contained about 30 acres of arable) were each said to be held by two tenants: 'Alfred and Robert hold one yardland' reads a typical entry in the survey of *c.* 1170.[16] At some recent time the single yardland holdings had been divided, perhaps between brothers, which suited the interests of peasant families who wished younger sons to have an inheritance, and the lord who thereby gained more tenants. A similar tendency affected the demesnes which were no doubt worked with efficiency by the lords of the smaller manors. The transfer of *Holeway* from the management of royal officials to the Cistercians probably led to an increase in its demesne's productivity.

Assarting, especially in the thirteenth century, accounted for the main increase in production. A couple of assarts only are mentioned in the survey of *c.* 1170, and lists of purprestures of about the same time show that crofts and *worths* were being enclosed from the waste, but again describe only two parcels of assarts. When Richard I exempted the bishopric from the penalties of assarting in 1189, Hanbury's share of a total for the whole estate of 614 cleared acres was only 34½ acres.[17] In the thirteenth century we can recognize an assarting campaign on four fronts: to the east from central

Hanbury and Broughton; southwards towards Goosehill; to the north from *Holeway*, and in a westward direction from Blickley, converging on the royal Park (see fig. 5).

The central strip of the parish (zone B in fig. 5) was probably at least partly cultivated before 1200, but still gave considerable scope for assarting. Its western edge is marked by the line of roads, including the Grenewey, which ran northwards from Broughton to the church. This boundary line was perambulated in 1300 by a band of local worthies who were claiming to re-establish the limits of Feckenham Forest as they had been before the reign of Henry II (see fig. 1).[18] They could not have known the old boundary, but were rather effecting a compromise between the king, who was willing to give up some forest but not all of it, and his subjects who wished the forests to be as small as possible. It is quite likely that they were following a real division that was still visible in the landscape between an area of old settlement to the west, and one of recent colonization to the east. Certainly the eastern area had seen much assarting in the thirteenth century: both the lord and the peasants of Broughton fell foul of the forest courts in 1262, 1270 and 1280; the substantial free tenant at the Mere in 1299 held a Ruding; the bishop's demesne included a Ruding and a Stocking; and the glebe also contained a Stocking (both Ruding and Stocking were names for land that had been cleared of trees); and to the north of the church Thomas Schad made an enclosure before 1276 to build his house.[19] The same boundary of 1300 ran along the Shell Brook through *Holeway* (see fig. 1) and it is likely that in a similar pattern some assarting continued north of that line in the thirteenth century, but in the absence of detailed documentation there is no supporting evidence for this conjecture.

Assarting was concentrated most intensely in the south-west and north-east (zone C in fig. 5), best recorded in the case of Blickley. Here there was some uncertainty, expressed in early thirteenth-century charters conveying land around the Berte Brook (later the Seeley Brook) and a place known as *Smalrugg*, about whether Blickley belonged to Hanbury or to Bradley, itself a woodland appendage of Fladbury. A charter of about 1220 conveyed Fladbury mill together with an assart in Blickley.[20] This problem is likely to have arisen from intercommoning arrangements whereby a large wooded area had been shared by the two manors. The definition of boundaries proceeded in the first 20 years of the thirteenth century, when two charters gave detailed descriptions of the limits of the land conveyed, and a third stated that a new purpresture would be perambulated by 12 free and legal men.[21] By 1299 19 tenants at Blickley held 11 assarts among other lands, in a virtually new settlement.[22]

The enclosure and clearance of land continued in the early fourteenth century. In 1306 the bishop was given permission to improve 300 acres in Hanbury and Blickley, and in pursuit of this goal grants of waste were made in 1307–18 in the northern area of common pasture at Prior's Longdon, and in the east between *Knottenhull* and Blickley.[23] Although the full 300 acres were not developed, by the middle of the fourteenth century tracts of uncultivated land were confined to the Park, the two wooded areas in the north and south-west, and the common grazing east of the church (zone D in fig. 5). In all at least a thousand acres of new land were cleared at Hanbury in the thirteenth century. Who did this work? The lords are often assumed to have been primarily responsible, and certainly impressively large acreages were assarted by the bishop in the 1270s, notable 100½ acres at the Ruding, and rather earlier Bordesley Abbey had cleared at least 120 acres at *Knottenhull*.[24] The bishops also organized the activities of others when they parcelled out pieces of waste in the early fourteenth century. However, this took place when the bishops felt a pressing need for extra income and at a time when the assarters may have needed some encouragement. There are earlier signs of tenants taking the initiative, and the role of the lord was merely to buy the already cleared land. Henry of Goosehill, a substantial freeholder, sold 45 acres at Goosehill to Bishop Cantilupe at some time between 1236 and 1266, and the demesne field of Bishop's Stocking was at least partly purchased.[25] Dozens of peasants were fined in the forest courts for offences against the vert, like William at the Marlpit of Blickley and Hawisia the widow who in 1270 were said to have assarted anew 3 perches of land.[26] Peasant clearances, though individually small in size, accounted cumulatively for a large area. Some peasants are recorded as holding no land other than an assart, and have the air of lone pioneers, creating their own livelihood from the waste. Others, like the members of the Wynter and Davy families, were tenants of customary half-yardlands. Their motives may sometimes have been to add to the total resources of their holdings, but more often they acquired extra land in order to provide for children who would not inherit the main family tenement. So we find three female members of the Wynter family, Juliana, Joan and Christina, holding small assarts in 1299, presumably as gifts from their father.[27]

All of this reflects a strong demand for land and high land values. The campaign of clearance cannot be separated from the commercial growth of the thirteenth century. The tenants of assarts were prepared to pay 1s per acre to the king for their offence against forest law, on top of payments such as 6d per acre to their lord. The purchase price paid by bishops to acquire land in assarting districts included such substantial sums as 20 marks (£13 6s 8d) for land at Blickley in 1218–19, and 25 marks (£16 13s 4d) at Goosehill in the mid-thirteenth century.[28] The story is not entirely of profit, however. Some assarters may have been willing to sell because of their financial difficulties. Clearing new land required heavy expenses in hedging and ditching as well as the removal of trees, and the land may not have always repaid the effort. A minority of peasant offenders were let off their fines by the forest courts on the grounds of their poverty.[29]

Finally, is it possible to explain the assarting movement in terms of the environment? The normal expectation is that the good land was used first and the poorer soils colonized only in times of land hunger. It is true that much of zone A consisted of red loams and clays of the Whimple 3 association, and that much of zone C coincides with the grey clay soils over Jurassic clay shales which are judged to be of inferior quality (see p. 10). However, most of zone B in central Hanbury, much of which was not assarted until the thirteenth century, is indistinguishable in its soils from the old-settled land further west, and Goosehill, also late settled, includes a considerable area of

the better land according to the modern judgements. Also, we must wonder
if the land was selected for the Park on the rational basis that its clay soils and
high ground made it doubly unsuitable for cultivation, or whether the choice
was made for the convenience of its royal users, who were motivated by the
pursuit of pleasure, not economic gain. As we have already noted, a sequence
of settlement which works in the case of Hanbury is not found throughout
the West Midland region, where the grey clays of the Evesham 2 and
Denchworth associations supported the corn-growing villages of the Vale of
Evesham and the Warwickshire Feldon in the high Middle Ages.

THE SETTLEMENTS IN THEIR PRIME

The proliferation of manors was accompanied by a multiplication of manor
houses and other high-status settlements (fig. 6). Nowhere is this more

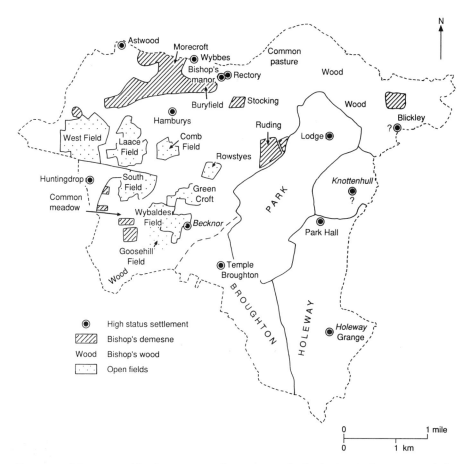

Figure 6 Manors and high-status settlements, with the bishop's demesne and the
open fields.

apparent than on Church Hill, which became crowded with buildings. The parish church has been much rebuilt, leaving no trace of the earlier minster. An addition of an aisle to the nave in the early thirteenth century may be connected with the increase in revenues and the growing number of parishioners at that time.[30] Nearby stood the rectory, the residence of a cleric with a wealthy living, which was often held by absentees, or clergy who employed assistants to carry out the parochial duties. These may well have lived on the hill, as did a chantry priest who was provided with land for a house by Bishop Giffard in 1287.[31] The bishop's manor house occupied the remainder of the hilltop. In the late fourteenth century it included a barn, granary and byre as well as a hall and chamber; near the *curia* lay a garden and spinney.[32] Away from the hill the bishop's sheepcote was sited near the common pasture towards Longdon, and more agricultural buildings stood in the *curia* at Blickley.

The most prestigious building in Hanbury lay in the Park, namely the Lodge which was used by hunting parties travelling from the main royal residence at Feckenham. Great Lodge Farm stands on the site next to a large fish pond, and another pond lies in the south of the Park. The ponds, and presumably the buildings, attracted much expenditure in the late twelfth century, and in 1393 Richard II authorized the use of stone from the then ruined house at Feckenham to repair the Lodge.[33] Smaller manor houses could still be elaborate structures. Hamburys, which has now disappeared under the modern Hanbury Hall or its gardens, consisted of a hall, great chamber, 'a little solar above the hall porch', stable and kitchen.[34] It may have been surrounded by a moat. The moat of Huntingdrop is still visible, and that of *Becknor* survives in an eroded form at Broughton Court, with a rectangular enclosure attached for farm buildings. Park Hall consisted of a platform measuring 70 by 40 metres, surrounded by a deep rectangular moat, which was fed and drained by a system of water channels that also filled a pond and small tanks for fish (fig. 7).[35] Lesser platforms show that some buildings stood outside the moated enclosure. One might expect that such a complex of structures was supported by a large estate, but there is no need to suppose that the holders were ever more than minor gentry; the manor was leased in the early sixteenth century for £5 per annum at a time when a gentleman ideally needed £10 annually to maintain his status.[36] The site of *Holeway* grange survived until 1982 (fig. 8). It consisted of a rectangular area of holloways and building platforms, covering an area of 6 acres. It contained space for a complex of agricultural buildings, yards and paddocks. At one stage of its history its southern boundary expanded over an area of adjacent arable land. After its destruction, debris on the site showed that buildings had stone foundations and roofs of ceramic tiles. Finds include a good deal of ironwork, such as a knife and chisel, and a great quantity of iron slag revealed that a forge had been worked on the site. It had been occupied during the twelfth, thirteenth and fourteenth centuries, judging from surace finds of pottery.

The location of these important settlements was influenced by considerations of status. The earlier use of the Church Hill site for a hill-fort and minster helped to determine that the bishop's manor and rectory stood there,

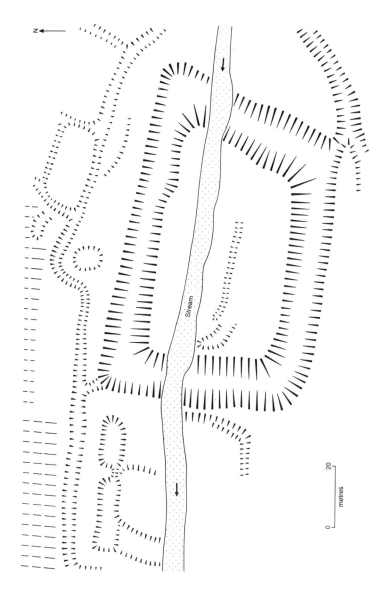

Figure 7   Moated site of Park Hall. The moat encloses a platform on which domestic buildings would have stood. The modern stream has been cut through the moat. Originally water flowed into the moat at its south-east corner, and out again in the north-west. Alternatively the flow of water bypassed the moat along the channel to the north. The water filled a large pond west of the moat (not shown) and also fed two tanks for fish, which are visible immediately to the west of the moat. Beyond the moat to the north are ridge and furrow (on the western side) and a series of rectangular enclosures which probably mark the sites of agricultural buildings.

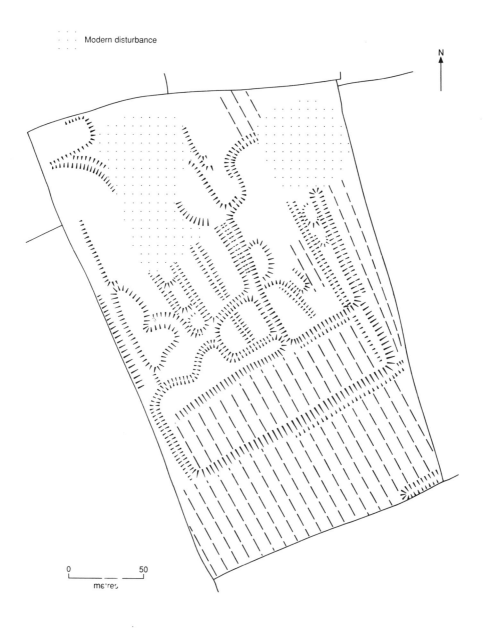

Modern disturbance

N

0   50
meres

Figure 8   Earthworks on the site of *Holeway* grange. The site is much disturbed by modern dumping to the north, but a series of holloways and ditches occupy a large area in the centre of the field, surrounding yards and at least nine rectangular platform for buildings. The southern edge was marked by a prominent lynchet. At some stage the area enclosed seems to have been extended southwards over former ridge and furrow. The ridge and furrow is preserved within the extension – perhaps the new enclosure was used as a pen for animals.

though it must have made an inconvenient centre for agricultural management. The depth of the holloway leading to the hilltop is a witness to the constant traffic of carts, wains and animals that made their journeys there, as well as the stream of tenants and parishioners. The dominating situation, together with a conservative desire to cling to the ancient site, must have kept it as the secular and religious centre of the parish. Temple Broughton manor, the Lodge, and *Holeway* grange also stood on rising ground. The lesser manors, such as *Becknor*, Hamburys, Huntingdrop and Park Hall all occupied low-lying positions, though they enjoyed the advantage of water supplies and could therefore enhance the status of the houses with moats.[37] Many of these high-grade settlements had as a common characteristic their marginal sites. They are ranged along the northern boundary of the parish, or along the edge of the Park, leaving western and central Hanbury for agricultural land and peasant settlements (fig. 6).

There were no nucleated villages at Hanbury. The word 'vill' was used in the documents to describe the whole parish, as for example when the vill of Hanbury paid its taxes to the king. The same term could be applied to the constituent parts of the parish: Astwood, Blickley, Broughton, Goosehill and Huntingdrop were all called vills at some time, and in the thirteenth century *Holeway* was described as a hamlet.[38] These terms referred simply to a territory, to identify the location of a house or field, and only in the case of Broughton is there clear evidence of a separate township having some form of collective responsibility for the management of fields and the presentment of cases to courts.[39]

The earthworks of now abandoned sites gives us some impression of the form of peasant messuages, the term used in documents for the whole complex of houses, farm buildings, yards and gardens. The messuage was usually inhabited by a single family and stood alone beside a road or lane. It was surrounded by a ditch or bank; the roughly rectangular enclosed area usually measured between 30 and 80 metres in length (fig. 9). Rectangular platforms suggest the presence of two or three buildings: a dwelling-house and a barn, and another building, either accommodation for animals or a bakehouse.[40] Sunken areas mark the sites of yards, and we can envisage a garden plot at the rear. Beyond the boundary ditch often lay the ridge and furrow of cultivated land.

In order to reconstruct the settlement pattern of the Middle Ages, we need to gather information from earthworks, pottery scatters, documents and maps, and all of these have been used to compile fig. 10. It includes the known roads, again based on both field evidence and the documents. All of the roads and houses marked on the maps of 1731–2 and 1591 have been included. Given the sources, some of the information will be inaccurate. Earthworks are undatable, and some of the roads and house sites marked on the early maps could have been newly built in the sixteenth and seventeenth centuries.[41] However, the main innovation in the landscape, the construction of Hanbury Hall and the creation of its new park on former arable land, was a recent event in 1731–2, and the older arrangements are still visible on the Dougharty map. Fig. 10 doubtless contains errors of detail, but the overall picture reflects the medieval landscape. The overwhelming impression is of a

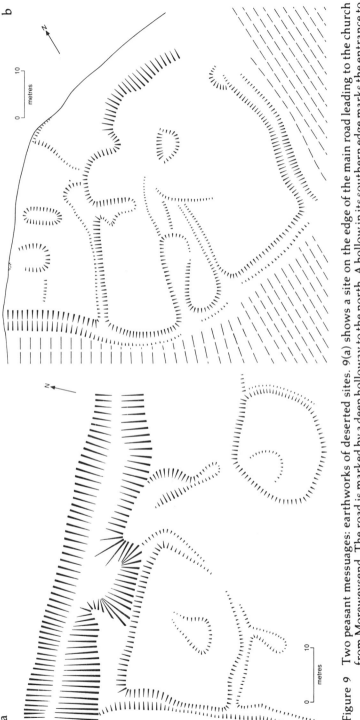

Figure 9   Two peasant messuages: earthworks of deserted sites. 9(a) shows a site on the edge of the main road leading to the church from Moreweysend. The road is marked by a deep holloway to the north. A hollow in its southern edge marks the entrance to the messuage. The depression to the east could be part of a yard, and the rectangular platform to the west is probably the site of one or two buildings, surrounded by a shallow ditch. The other platform to the south-east may also have carried buildings. 9(b) This messuage stood at the junction of the medieval Grenewey and the road now called Pumphouse Lane. The depression to the west probably marks the entrance from the road. The area of the toft or messuage is surrounded by a ditch, beyond which lies the ridge and furrow. Two rectangular platforms in the centre of the site mark the site of buildings, and the large rectangular area to the east was probably used as a yard or garden. For location see fig. 11.

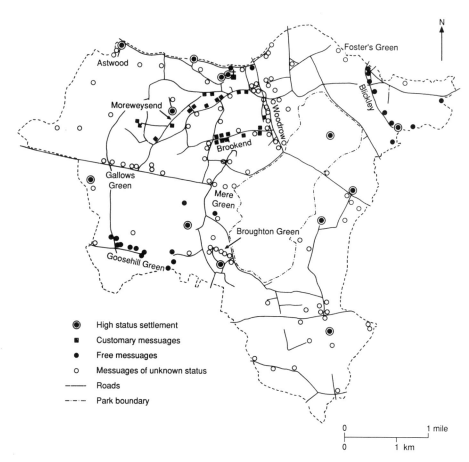

Figure 10   Medieval roads and settlements at their maximum extent, *c.* 1300. Based
on a combination of archaeological and documentary evidence, and
making much use of the maps of 1731–2 and 1591.

close network of roads covering the whole parish except the Park, which was
crossed by a single route in 1591.[42] The houses are sited on the roads,
sometimes, as at Woodrow, in an almost continuous succession, but more
often with intervals between. The messuages cluster notably in the centre of
the parish between the Roman road and the church. Blickley, Broughton and
Goosehill have lesser concentrations.

The documents allow us to assign many of the messuages to groups, called
'ends' (Moreweysend and Brookend towards the centre of the parish, and
Churchend which is rarely mentioned), and 'greens' at Broughton, Goosehill,
Mere Green and Woodrow. Blickley also belongs to the green category and
there were other small greens: Gallows Green near Huntingdrop, and
Foster's Green in the north-east. These groups will be examined in more
detail.

Moreweysend can be traced from the messuage of Moreweys on the edge

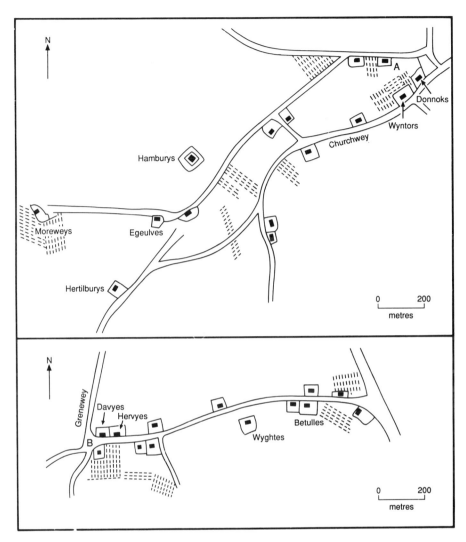

Figure 11 Morweysend (top) and Brookend (bottom): a reconstruction. These plans
are based on archaeological, documentary and map evidence, and involve
conjecture. A and B mark the location of the sites shown in fig. 9.

of Laace Field (fig. 11). Houses can be seen on either side of two roads, one
called Churchwey, leading north-eastward towards the church. Two of them
to the south, Hertilburys and Egeulves or Eggeolfes can be identified from
maps, and to the west stood the grander house of Hamburys, the site of
which is now occupied by Hanbury Hall. Near the church Wyntors and
Donnoks survive as earthworks. Some of the other messuages were Elvyns,
Colmans, Duryans and others, which cannot be identified with certainty, but
must now exist as sites marked by earthworks and scatters of pottery. Other
messuages like Brewtors stood nearer to the church. Brookend (fig. 11)
survives in skeletal form along the modern Pumphouse Lane. The rental of

1466 begins with Davyes and Hervyes and these are known to have stood at the junction with the Grenewey or Grene Street. Wyghtes and Betulles are also known, and are mentioned towards the end of the Brookend section of the rental, and the messuages such as Annes and Lynnes, Waves, Bredons and Fortheyes must have occupied the sites in between, three of which are marked by modern houses, five by earthworks, and two by dense scatters of pottery. Wyghtes is shown on the map a little to the south of the modern White House because a scatter of pottery suggests its site has shifted. In all perhaps a dozen messuages were distributed along a stretch of road about ¾ mile (1 km) long.

The pattern revealed by our examination of the two 'ends' recurs in other parts of the parish, and indeed in other areas of dispersed settlement in Worcestershire and beyond. The houses or messuages are arranged along a road on both sides, either in isolation or in pairs. They lay some 100 to 300 yards apart, separated by a croft or a piece of arable land, now indicated by ridge and furrow. This arrangement has such a distinctive form, that it is best described as an interrupted row. This involves applying to non-nucleated settlements the term 'row', which was used in the Middle Ages and is now employed by modern morphologists to describe the line of houses along a village street.[43]

The green settlements at Hanbury, like those elsewhere, bore some resemblance to the ends, in the sense that the houses ran in interrupted rows, but they tended to form a single line, sometimes along a road passing through a green or strip of common pasture (as at Goosehill Green), or the houses were arranged round the edge of the green, as at Mere Green and Broughton Green (fig. 10). Woodrow in central Hanbury was of the former type, with all of its houses on the western side of the main north–south road, and although Blickley was not called a green, its messuages lay along the common separating Berte Brook from the woods to the west.[44] When the green took the form of a belt of pasture separating the arable fields from woods, the settlements are given the appearance of the last wave of an advancing tide of clearance (see fig. 10).

Not all settlements were grouped into ends, rows and greens. The house (or perhaps two) recorded at Uppington, the site now marked by a scatter of pottery, stood alone between the common arable fields of Greencroft and Wybaldesfield.[45] Thomas Schad's house behind the church has already been mentioned, and small knots of houses are recorded in the documents at Huntingdrop, and as earthworks at Astwood.[46]

The wider meaning of these settlement patterns deserves careful consideration. The ends seem to have formed at an earlier date than the greens. Moreweysend belongs in the part of western Hanbury that was fully developed by 1086 (see fig. 5) and Brookend ran from that zone of early settlement into the central belt that had been at least partially settled before the thirteenth century, whereas Goosehill Green and Blickley grew in the phase of large-scale assarting in the thirteenth century. The differences are underlined by the contrasting types of tenure found in the different settlements. The majority of the messuages of customary holdings, that is those held in villeinage in the thirteenth century, were concentrated in the central area, in the 'ends'.[47] Some free tenements were interspersed with those of the villeins, but most free messuages were to be found in the north around the church, and in the assarting settlements such as Blickley and Goosehill. The names of the messuages derive from the surnames of the peasant families who held them in the thirteenth and fourteenth centuries. Some of the families go back before 1200, and it is tempting to suggest that just as Roger de Hembury, who appears in the survey of *c.* 1170, lived on the high-status holding that was eventually to be called Hamburys, so the peasants who appear in the same survey called Idwy Wynter, Robert Perler, Herewy and Eggulf were also living at that time in the messuages that appear in later documents and maps as Wyntors, Parlers, Hervyes and Eggeolfes. Such an argument depends on a rather static view of medieval society. Archaeological work on settlements reveals that they often changed their sites, and historical studies of the land market show that families did not always cling to the same holding from generation to generation.[48] This makes it less probable that the twelfth-century Idwy Wynter really lived at the house south of the church, which we know from later records to have been called Wyntors. But it still seems likely that these people occupied the same part of the parish, and that the ends represent the areas of relatively old settlement.

The messuages in the ends are not distributed at random, but form an orderly pattern along the roads. A tempting argument might be to link this with their customary status, and to think that as the *villani* of the eleventh century probably lived here, they had begun as the houses of *buri* or *geburs* (boors) settled on the demesne by pre-Conquest lords.[49] The survey of *c.* 1170 supports this supposition by stating that six of the yardlands owing labour services were *de dominico* (of the demesne). Perhaps the lord's officials laid out this settlement. However, the ends were not peopled entirely by tenants of servile origin – the de Hanburys lived in Moreweysend, for example. The greens also, which were mainly free settlements in which the lord had less influence, were not entirely anarchic in their plan. As far as can be seen, Blickley, for instance resembled an end except that the houses lay in one line. In any case, there are great difficulties in attempting to discern an 'original' plan when the pattern must have changed. To take one element of development, the survey of *c.* 1170 records the division of yardlands into half-yardlands, and therefore presumably messuages were split at the same time. The occasional appearance of pairs of messuages may well recall that process.

The grouping of the customary tenants in the ends, and the tendency of the high-status settlements and the messuages of freeholders to lie on the margins, together with the proliferation of freeholdings on the outer fringes when the new lands were being developed, made for a striking social segregation. Did this affect social relationships within the village? Did the free inhabitants of the outer ring look down on the people of the central zone of unfree villeins?

Settlements functioned in relation to their agricultural resources, and the messuages cannot be separated from the land. A common belief is that the cultivators in nucleated villages worked strips scattered over the open fields, while the inhabitants of the woodlands had their lands more conveniently concentrated around their houses. Only some of Hanbury's landholders enjoyed this advantage. Certainly at an early stage of the development of the demesne the lord could exploit a compact belt of land that began at Buryfield near Church Hill and ran westward to the Body Brook (fig. 6). Not only were the fields contiguous, but both the arable and meadow lay conveniently together. Pasture was available nearby to the east on the common. Only the woodland resources were remote from the manor house. With the assarting movement and the growth of the land market, thirteenth-century bishops decided to expand the demesne. This must be regarded as rather an unusual policy as nowhere else on the estate did the demesne arable grow from an area worked by two ploughs to one cultivated by five. Perhaps Hanbury alone among the bishop's manors gave opportunities for such a move. As the available new land lay on the edges of the manor, at Goosehill, near the Park and at Blickley, the demesne took on a scattered form, though in each case the bishop's land lay in discrete blocks, not in interspersed strips. In addition to the arable, meadow was acquired at both Goosehill and Blickley, and enclosed pasture also at Blickley.[50] Compact demesnes are found in the east of Hanbury, where, judging from descriptions at the time of the Dissolution, *Holeway* grange was provided with blocks of land called Low Field and Brook Field.[51] The monks of Bordesley joined in the assarting movement, with typical Cistercian rationality, by founding a new grange at *Knottenhull*, surrounded by its own lands. Park Hall, the lay manor sandwiched between the two granges, also formed a compact estate.

By contrast the lesser manors and substantial freeholdings consisted of complex parcels of lands widely scattered over the parish, or at least that is how they appear in documents of the fifteenth and sixteenth centuries. The glebe, for example, is first fully recorded at 140½ acres in 1585, but is likely to have had much earlier origins.[52] It included strips of arable in West Field and Laace Field, and fields such as Pegenhull and Stocking near the Park. Evidently an enterprising thirteenth-century rector either directed some assarting himself, or acquired land from those who had carried out large-scale clearance. Hamburys and Wybbes combined holdings of strips in open fields with scattered crofts and parcels.[53] Hamburys in the fifteenth century included assets as far apart as Astwood, South Field and Blickley (fig. 6).

The customary holdings were provided with crofts and sometimes strips of arable near their messuages. In 1428 Wyntors was described as 'a toft and half yardland . . . with four selions adjacent'.[54] The site of this messuage is still visible, and adjoining the platforms and ditches of the house and yards there is indeed an area of ridge and furrow. The bordlands, forelands and swinelands held by customary tenants may also have lain near to the messuages, and these terms seem to refer to parcels lying outside the main open fields. However, much of the arable of the half-yardland tenements was distributed in strips in the open fields, and they held shares in the common meadow near Goosehill. Hertilburys in 1466, for example, was linked with land in Green Croft, Wybaldes Field, and Walleshey.[55] The strips of each holding were unevenly distributed over a number of open fields, and the peasants of the ends must have travelled at least as many miles to their lands as did anyone living in a nucleated village.

Free tenants were more likely to hold enclosed parcels near their houses. A small freeholding was often described as 'a messuage with a certain adjacent croft'. Many had no land in the open fields, though they often held parcels of common meadow. Some large freeholdings lay in single blocks, like the 'two fields called Lywyngesfeld' which contained much of John Beste's land in 1433, and the 'ruding' held by Cristina atte Mere in 1299.[56] Again these differences between customary holdings and freeholdings point to their distinct origins, the customary tenements having acquired at an early date shares in the long-cultivated open fields in west and south Hanbury, while the freeholders tended to have large parcels of newly cleared and enclosed land.

LAND USE AND AGRICULTURE IN THEIR PRIME

The organization of agricultural land at Hanbury follows a well-known woodland pattern. Some arable lay in irregular open fields, but much was in enclosures.[57] The proportion of arable rose in the twelfth and thirteenth centuries, though even at its maximum extent it still left larger areas under grass or wood than is found in champion districts.

The terminology used to describe fields is inconsistent, in that 'field' could mean an enclosed parcel, as well as a large area of subdivided arable, and the term 'croft' could sometimes be applied not just to a small enclosure but also to an area of open field. The open-field arable lay in a belt of land running from west to east along the Roman road, in West Field, Laace Field, Combe Field and Rowstyes Field, to the north of the road, and South Field, Wybaldes Field, Goosehill Field and Green Croft to the south (fig. 6). There were also forelands, bordlands and swinelands, arable that had not been absorbed into the main fields. Much of the rest of the land lay in numerous crofts. A rental of 1410 mentions 37, and that was not intended to be a complete list.[58] The open fields, together with the western part of the bishop's demesne, represent the area of old cultivation, while many of the crofts were created during the assarting campaign of the thirteenth century. For example, the numerous crofts at Blickley probably totalled 150 acres, and at Goosehill a ditch marked the frontier between 'Goosehill Field and *les crofts*'.[59] This argument should not be taken too far, because crofts could be very old, as is shown by references to them as boundary points in pre-Conquest charters, especially in north Worcestershire, and some of the Hanbury crofts, like Donnokscroft, were probably as old as this. And there was clearly a process by which crofts could change into open field. For example, the eastern open fields Rowstyes and Wybaldes, carry the names of individuals, so that at some time they were presumably held as separate parcels but were then subdivided by inheritance, the splitting of tenures or the land market. Green Croft in view of its 'croft' name is likely to have had a similar origin.[60]

The management of the arable was clearly not based on simple divisions of land like the conventional two and three-field systems of the champion. The fields were numerous, and the selions or strips of which they were composed appear to have been irregularly distributed among the tenants. A holding described in 1407 consisted of 7 selions in South Field and 3 selions in West Field.[61] None the less, the fields were subject to agreed rotations which allowed regular fallowing of the land. Grazing on the stubble was practised after the harvest and during the year that land lay fallow. The fields were surrounded by hedges and fences, with gaps that were supposed to be filled once the crops had been planted. Wybaldes Field was enclosed on one side by a ditch 4 feet wide.[62] The bylaws governing the cropping regime are not recorded until the fifteenth century, but must reflect earlier practice. In 1474, for example, South Field and Wybaldes Field were designated the winter field, and in 1489 Combe Field and Lance Field served as the spring field;[63] but the precise rationale behind such arrangements is difficult to reconstruct.

Common grazing extended beyond the area of open field. Land held in severalty in crofts, as well as the demesne and the glebe, were supposed to be open after the harvest and in the fallow year. There were also large areas of permanent grass available for common pasture, over the meadows after the hay harvest, and on the many greens. The main common pasture lay north-east of Woodrow and included Longdon on the steeply sloping side of Forest Hill; it must have accounted for at least 300 acres (fig. 12). The extension of the arable in the thirteenth century stopped on wet ground unsuitable for cultivation, leaving large areas for use as meadow, notably on the common meadow north of Goosehill, but also along the minor streams in the centre of the parish and in the valleys of the brooks both to the west and the east. Meadow must always have been in excess of 300 acres.

The royal Park also made some contribution to the pasture resources of the parish. On the map of 1591 it appears to be divided into compartments, containing both areas of wood and lawns for the deer.[64] An indication of the size of the deer herd at a late stage of its history is given by the statement in 1503 that 260 animals had died of disease. The Park was large enough to support four times that number.[65] However, it was put to more practical use. In the later twelfth century pigs were pastured there, and in 1177–8 the pannage payments totalled 8s 1d, showing that a hundred or more animals were feeding on the acorns.[66] Judging from the constant complaints in the thirteenth-century forest courts of trespass in the Park, it is likely that Hanbury people were able to make some illicit use of its grazing.

The woods of the bishop and the other lords accounted for a great deal of land. Down Wood in the north required a mile and a quarter (377 perches) of fencing in 1431–2, and that was not for a complete circuit, and Mawdittsrow towards Blickley was provided with ¾ mile of fencing in 1448–9.[67] Goosehill Wood probably covered 100 acres, together with smaller woods in western Hanbury at Westall and Walling Croft.[68] Bordesley Abbey's wood at *Knottenhull* amounted to 185 acres in 1362, and there were unknown quantities in *Holeway* and Broughton.[69] To allow the coppice wood to grow for fuel for the Droitwich salt-works, these were often enclosed, thus preventing grazing within the woods. Substantial trees were grown as well–the bishops could raise large sums in a hurry by selling off the timber. Some of the woods were managed as wood-pasture: Goosehill Wood in 1299 was described as 'trunks and underwood' providing food for 'cattle and pigs without number' for those 'both villein and free' who had common rights.[70] Tenants had access to some of the woods in the fifteenth century, when there were complaints of their 'hewing and hacking' at night-time; they were allowed a limited number of trees for fuel and building.[71] Their messuages and crofts were surrounded by hedgerows from which hawthorn, oaks, elm and ash were taken for use or sale.

In addition to the major agricultural resources of the parish, damp valley bottoms could be put to some use, like the Hambury family's withy-bed recorded in 1436. There were no less than six sets of fish ponds (fig. 12).[72] Three of these, at Hanbury Hall, Swancombe and the Stews at Broughton may have had medieval origins but were remodelled in more recent times. The ponds associated with Park Hall were certainly in use at the same time as the moat, and the two sets of royal ponds in the Park are well documented. Much money was spent on them in the 1160s and 1170s, and the pond near Great Lodge, which still retains its massive dam, was repaired in 1393–4 with stone from a demolished chapel at Bentley at a cost of £49.[73] These ponds cannot be regarded as a local asset however, as they formed part of a royal network from which fish were drawn for the provisioning of the household.[74] Their only significance for Hanbury people would have been as a source of occasional employment, and as a venue for poaching expeditions.

It ought to be possible to calculate the proportions of land given over to arable, meadow, pasture and wood. No document gives a full picture of land use, because wood was often omitted from surveys, or at least its area was not given, and common pastures, if mentioned at all, were assessed in terms of the numbers of animals that could be kept. The figures in Table 2 give

Table 2. Land use at Hanbury, 1290–1362, in acres[75]

Estate and date	Arable	Meadow	Pasture	Wood	Total
Hanbury demesne	317	45¼	13⅞	–	376⅛
c. 1290	84%	12%	4%	–	100%
Blickley demesne	98⅜	10¼	51⅞	–	160½
c. 1290	62%	6%	32%	–	100%
Hanbury and Goose-					
hill demesne	378½	37	34 †	–	449½
1299	84%	8%	8%	–	100%
Blickley demesne	103 *	9½	16	–	128½
1299	80%	7%	13%		100%
Knottenhull grange	120	10	24	185	339
1362	35%	3%	7%	55%	100%
Kyng's tenement					
Blickley	40	6	–	–	46
1356	87%	13%			100%

Notes
† and pasture for 300 sheep in summer
* half is 'frisc', i.e. uncultivated

higher proportions of meadow and pasture than are often found in medieval surveys, and therefore reflect the significance of animal husbandry in Hanbury's economy; in each case we must make an additional allowance for the unenclosed pasture.[76]

Fig. 12 reconstructs the use of land in the parish at the maximum extent of cultivation in the late thirteenth century. It is based on the early maps which show the Park and its internal divisions, and the areas of common pasture and greens. The medieval documents also name fields and indicate their use. Modern arable fields with thin scatters of medieval pottery found in field-walking are another guide to the cultivation of land (see p. 16). To some extent gaps have been filled by observation of ridge and furrow from ground-level survey and aerial photographs. Often the physical and documentary evidence duplicate each other. The area of open fields, especially those north of the Roman road, is filled with ridge and furrow of distinctive type, with rather narrow ridges between 4 and 6 metres wide. In the southern part of the parish, the areas known to have been arable fields in the Middle Ages, in Brook Field, Down Field and Low Field, there is an abundance of ridge and furrow, often with rather wider ridges, nearer the normal size in the Midlands, of between 6 and 9.6 metres. A wider ridge is also recorded at Goosehill and Ditchford (Blickley) which might suggest a link between the width of ridges and the date at which the land came under the plough. However the dating of ridge and furrow is always a problem, especially in a parish where arable cultivation continued into modern times. Much of the surviving ridge and furrow is likely to have been ploughed until the eighteenth century, and its latest use may have determined the form in which it now survives. Occasionally we can be confident of a date for its last cultivation. For example, there are large areas of narrow ridge and furrow in the park around Hanbury Hall, which must have gone out of ploughing before about 1700. Sometimes the ridge and furrow associated with deserted settlements would appear to have been abandoned along with the houses in the period 1350–1500. Some of the ridge and furrow poses problems because it seems to contradict the evidence of the documents. We do not expect to find medieval cultivation in the Park or on the site of the woods but there are more than 130 acres of ridge and furrow recorded in the southern part of the Park, and at least 30 acres on the site of Down Wood. We could reject the physical evidence, by presuming that these areas were permanently closed to cultivation in the Middle Ages, and that therefore this ridge and furrow must have been formed when these areas were given over to agriculture in the seventeenth and eighteenth centuries. The other possibility is that the woods and the Park were not managed inflexibly, and that at times when it seemed profitable the royal and bishop's officials allowed the local peasants to clear and till an area. There are many other examples of temporary cultivation in parks, though this would not explain the high-backed ridges found near Broughton Wood, which had clearly been cultivated for a long period, and one must suspect there that the boundary between the Park and Temple Broughton has at some time been changed.

The field evidence can sometimes give us an insight into medieval agriculture which is not conveyed by the documents. The practice of marling the fields with subsoil obtained from deep pits is only occasionally mentioned in written sources. The surname 'at the marl pit' occurs in thirteenth-century Blickley, and pits are once or twice mentioned as boundary marks in deeds, but otherwise the only indication of marling on any considerable scale was the complaint in 1456 that Thomas Bearcroft had dug a pit in the common way under Becknor Hill.[77] Not only does that pit survive as a large cavity near Mere Hall, but a total of 69 pits have been noted in the survey, often on the edge of areas of ridge and furrow. The application of marl was clearly an important technique for improving soil fertility, though again precise chronology eludes us.

Fig. 12 conveys an impression of a predominance of arable land. Indeed it does not include the whole arable area, because we can presume that some of the spaces left blank for lack of evidence were once cultivated, and as explained above, the arable shading ought perhaps to extend at least into the south-west corner of the Park. However, the map also omits a type of pasture which accounted for an important part of the grazing resources of the parish, that is on the often wide roadside verges, which in some places took on the

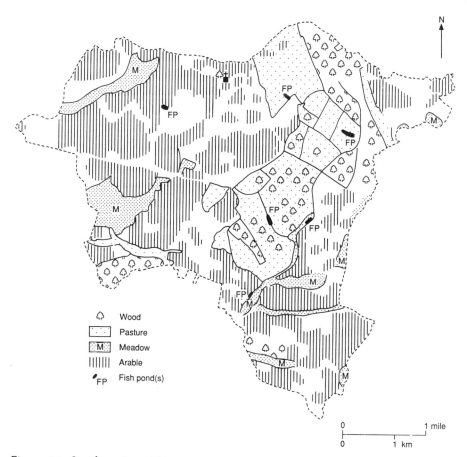

N

ᘐ	Wood
[∴]	Pasture
:M:	Meadow
‖‖‖	Arable
•FP	Fish pond(s)

0   1 mile

0   1 km

Figure 12   Land use in *c.* 1300.

character of narrow greens. Bearing in mind these uncertainties, and excluding the woods and Park, it seems reasonable to estimate that a fifth of the agricultural land in Hanbury was used as meadow and pasture.

The implication of this conclusion is that pasture resources had been severely restricted by the thirteenth-century assarting. Hanbury by 1300 was beginning to resemble a champion village in the balance of its agriculture, though the proportion of arable was still lower than that prevailing in many champion districts. The advance of cultivation is often represented as a progressive move, as if the wastes that were cleared and ploughed had no value. Of course the grazing-land was an important element in the economy, and in the eleventh and twelfth centuries, when the bulk of the central strip of the parish (zone B in fig. 5) was used as pasture, resources were healthily balanced. Not only were the inhabitants able to turn almost unlimited numbers of animals on to the commons, but these lands were easy of access, as everyone in the ends lived in close proximity to the edge of the thousand-acre common. When the common pasture was restricted to the northern end of the central belt, and the smaller remnants on the greens at Mere Green and Broughton Green, the peasants of the ends must have found their working lives absorbed by more travel, as the main area of pasture, as well as much of the open field, and the common meadow, lay ¾ mile (1 km) or more from their homes.

WOODLAND SOCIETY IN ITS PRIME

Late medieval woodlands had distinctive social characteristics. They were inhabited mainly by freeholders, who owed only light obligations to their lords. The seignorial regime of the woodland manors was less oppressive than that of the champion, partly because of the prevalence of lesser and weaker lords, such as members of the gentry. The lower densities of population freed the woodlanders from the restraints of strong village communities. They lived in isolated houses, away from interfering neighbours. They held lands in enclosures, and could use the land as arable or pasture, or employ whichever cropping system suited them best. The agrarian economy was biased towards the pastoral, partly because the land tended to be less fertile and less suited to cereal-growing, and partly because of the extensive commons. Smallholders proliferated, reflecting the busy land market, the tendency of freeholdings to fragment when a family failed to produce male heirs, and the small scale of land clearance. Pastoral farming was associated with a flexible style of living. The inhabitants had more free time, and a stronger market orientation than peasants committed to a heavy routine of ploughing and sowing. They were more likely than the inhabitants of champion villages to pursue non-agricultural occupations, taking advantage of the available time and the raw materials, especially the timber and fuel from the woods. Sometimes this was a necessity, because of the small size of their holdings. Their mentality tended to individualism and nonconformity: they turned more readily than the stolid champion peasants to rebellion and crime. The Robin Hood ballads express the romance, freedom, and disregard for conventional law typical of the dwellers in woodlands.[78]

The people of Hanbury fitted this pattern in many ways. In 1299, when English serfdom was at its height, only 38 of the 91 tenants on the bishop's manor held customary tenements which were burdened with labour service, marriage fines and the other disabilities of villeinage. The main obligation of the majority, the freeholders, was payment of a modest cash rent. If 60 per cent of the bishop's tenants were freeholders, we can take it that the other manors had at least as high a proportion. Besides the ancient ecclesiastical manor, Hanbury was dominated by lords more typical of the woodlands, lay gentry and the new religious foundations of the twelfth century, who tended to wield limited power over their peasants. After the growth in population the density of *c.* 1300 was not low, at about 60 people per square mile (23 per square km), but it was considerably less than those prevailing in most eastern and Midland counties.[79] The scattered settlements and individualistic management of land must have reduced the cohesion and power of the village community. Pastoral agriculture was practised by both lords and peasants. For example, Bordesley Abbey at *Knottenhull* in the mid-thirteenth century kept 20 oxen (more than was needed to cultivate the arable), 18 other cattle and 3 horses. Cristina de Dichforde, a peasant, is known at the same time to have owned at least 3 cattle and horses, 6 goats and 4 pigs.[80] The records of the royal forest mention cattle, goats and pigs most commonly, of which the goats seem especially characteristic of the woodland environment. They were discouraged in much of England because of the damage that they caused to the pasture and young trees, and in some places they were banned entirely. The Hanbury peasants could grow crops of flax, much reported in the fifteenth century, by ploughing up patches of common pasture, indicating the flexibility of the woodland agrarian system.[81] A number of field-names containing the element 'lin-' show that flax was grown in the early Middle Ages. Rules and customs were often broken. In 1376 the tenants of Blickley refused to contribute their headpenny to the bishop, perhaps a typical gesture of defiance from a remote woodland settlement.[82] Adam Salesbrugg stands out in the forest records as a notorious poacher, who was accused of taking the king's deer with nets on four occasions in 1370–4. Once he 'entered the king's park', 'with nets and other engines'. But he was only one of many Hanbury people who flouted forest law by taking trees, poaching deer and putting animals to graze even within the pale of the Park.[83]

Yet we must make some qualifications and reservations, because no example will accord entirely with the ideal type. The presence of a major ecclesiastical lord made a considerable impact, even on a woodland society. The servile half-yardlanders, who formed a sizeable minority of Hanbury's tenants, owed very heavy obligations to their lord. In theory, in 1299 they could be required to work on the demesne two days per week for much of the year, and on four days per week in the harvest. If this was converted in practice to cash rents, the total came to 11s per year, as high a figure as could be found on any champion manor on the bishop's estate.[84] Servile status was still being enforced at Hanbury at the end of the fourteenth century, and persisted into the fifteenth. Communal institutions cannot be underestimated, in view of the hundreds of acres of open field, and the widespread right to common pasture in the crofts and closes. The vigour of the village community is indicated by the continual issuing of bylaws in the manor courts in the fifteenth century, dealing, among other matters, with the maintenance of common grazing rights in enclosed land. The parish church played an important unifying role in this type of large and diffusely settled parish, especially at Hanbury in the absence of chapels-of-ease. The services and church ales must have been important gatherings which helped to create a sense of neighbourliness and common responsibility. Nor did the economy entirely fit with the woodland model. Arable cultivation played a dominant role in agriculture both for the demesne and for most of the peasants. The quality of the land seems to have been good enough for a high proportion of wheat to be grown, and quantities of peas and beans, as well as the oats often associated with woodland cultivation. Pastures were stinted, and over-burdening of commons was a problem even in the fifteenth century, when the area of grazing had increased. The numbers of animals mentioned in the forest records do not suggest that peasant flocks and herds were much larger than in the champion districts.[85] Smallholders predominated among the free tenants, but all of the customary tenants in 1299 held a minimum of a half-yardland of about 15 acres, so unless there were many sub-tenants unknown to us, Hanbury does not seem to have been overfilled with poor cottagers. This may be linked with the absence of industry. True, the documents of different periods mention a smith, and archaeological evidence of slag, coal and charcoal from Wyntors holding near the church suggests that a peasant forge was sited there, but many villages supported such a craftsman.[86] There was not even a miller for much of Hanbury's history, because the bishop's manor had no water-mill, and the windmill built in the thirteenth century soon fell down. Towards the end of the fifteenth century an enterprising peasant operated a horse-mill in his house.[87]

There is no way of judging the strength of Hanbury's peasants' involvement in buying and selling, though they must have had many opportunities for contact with Droitwich, which by the thirteenth century had taken on the character of a market town.[88] The growth of specialized retail trade within the village, epitomized by the rise of Henry Pugge and his wife as ale-housekeepers between 1441 and 1482, is a normal trend of the period. We know, like villagers everywhere, that they sold goods outside, like the horse and cart from Hanbury bought in 1391 by a peasant from Whitstones, 7 miles away.[89] Hanbury peasants brought goods from a distance, such as cast bronze cooking-pots and pottery vessels made at Worcester and Hanley Castle, though the purchases were probably made at Droitwich or Bromsgrove, or from itinerant peddlars.[90] They were not especially likely to migrate, as the turnover of tenants was rather lower than in other late medieval manors. Of the 20 surnames of customary tenants in 1410, eight had been current on the manor in 1299, and in the Hanbury court-rolls for 1375 to 1500, a period of almost habitual instability of population, quite a high proportion of transfers of land were between members of the same family, from 13 per cent in some decades to 40 per cent in others.[91] Nor can we say that the inhabitants of Hanbury were more prone to crime, though the forest did provide temptations, and an additional set of officials to collect evidence of wrongdoing. The Hanbury tenants' resistance to the lordship of the bishop can be paralleled throughout the estate, and on the manors of many other lords.

Chapter 4

Settlement Retreat, and New Beginnings

The discovery in the last 40 years of more than 2,000 deserted medieval villages in England has convincingly demonstrated the large scale of the settlement retreat in the fourteenth and fifteenth centuries. Now we are accumulating evidence of thousands of villages which shrank in size, and even larger numbers of depopulated hamlets and farmsteads.[1] The desertion of scattered settlements has been demonstrated from the south-western peninsula to Suffolk, and from the Sussex weald to the Yorkshire moors.[2] Behind this common tendency lay the drop in population in the later Middle Ages, from a national total of five or six million in 1300 to about three million in the early sixteenth century.[3] Hanbury suffered great losses in the Black Death epidemic and two-thirds of the holdings in the bishop's manor lay vacant in the autumn of 1349. Numbers recovered until the bishop's officials could list as many as 60 tenants in 1410, but they dwindled again to only 47 in 1544, about a half of the total in 1299.[4] In the whole parish, which has been estimated as supporting about 725 people in 1299, a population of only about 400 can be calculated from the muster of 1522 and the ecclesiastical census of 1563.[5] In such circumstances we can expect to find many houses falling into ruin and holdings becoming vacant, and this is indeed the case.

A possible explanation of these events is that Hanbury, in common with the rest of Europe, was afflicted by a Malthusian crisis. The countryside was burdened by an excessive weight of population; ineffective methods of cultivation, too much arable compared with pasture, and the colonization of poor marginal land left food in short supply. Hunger and famine reduced the population from the second decade of the fourteenth century, and the crisis deepened when the first plague caused a mortality near to 50 per cent, and was followed by a succession of epidemics.[6] Some of Hanbury's circumstances could conform with this interpretation. Its population in 1299 was not much lower than that of the nineteenth century (for example, 855 in 1891).[7] There were many freeholders in the late thirteenth century whose landholdings were too small to feed their families, and who must have suffered when grain prices rose in the bad harvest years of the 1290s and in the early fourteenth century. We know that a few miles to the north at Halesowen, a not dissimilar manor, 15 per cent of the male population died in the Great Famine of 1315–17.[8] The bishop of Worcester complained of Hanbury's 'poor land' in 1306, and attempts to let out parcels of waste seem to have petered out after 1318, perhaps because of reduced demand for land and the tenants' recognition of its low quality.[9] After the Black Death, Hanbury is known to have been afflicted by at least four lesser outbreaks of disease in the mid-fifteenth century, which would have helped to prevent any recovery of the population.[10] New lands were certainly abandoned during the retreat, such as the ten assarts said to have reverted to common in 1466, presumably because they did not repay cultivation.[11]

However, the weight of evidence does not entirely favour a Malthusian interpretation. Hanbury's density of population in the late thirteenth century was not high by the standards of lowland England, and pastures were still quite extensive. Smallholders cannot be regarded as numerous. Also, the quality of the newly colonized land was not perceived as poor by the bishops and monks who made their own clearances and purchased other people's assarts in the thirteenth century.

The survey of the settlements and their abandonment ought to enable us to test the argument that the lands that were colonized in the thirteenth century were so marginal in quality that they reverted to waste when settlement and cultivation retreated. The physical remains of earthworks and pottery scatters, combined with documentary evidence and maps enables us to locate 80 deserted messuages within the parish (fig. 13). They are not closely datable, either in their origin or their disappearance, but about half were deserted before 1731, the bulk of those in the later Middle Ages. There were others, perhaps as many as another 40, which are known from the documents to have ceased to be inhabited between 1300 and 1540 and which cannot be located precisely on the ground. The documents refer to messuages that had lost their buildings as 'tofts', and the proportion of holdings headed by empty tofts rather than built messuages rose from a third to almost a half during the fifteenth century. The topographically arranged rental of 1466 allows comparisons to be made between different parts of the bishop's manor (see table 3). It reveals no striking variation between the ends and the recently colonized settlement of Blickley; if anything the proportion was rather higher in the older settlements.

Table 3   Messuages and tofts in 1466

	Blickley		Moreweysend		Brookend	
Tofts	6	(50%)	12	(57%)	8	(66%)
Messuages	6	(50%)	9	(43%)	4	(33%)
TOTAL	12	(100%)	21	(100%)	12	(100%)

The deserted settlements in fig. 13 also cluster in the ends, so there is little support from either documents or archaeology for the theory that the areas of late settlement in the greens, where the colonizers had to struggle with the sticky grey clays, suffered the main brunt of the late medieval retreat.[12] This is not unexpected, as we have known for decades of the large-

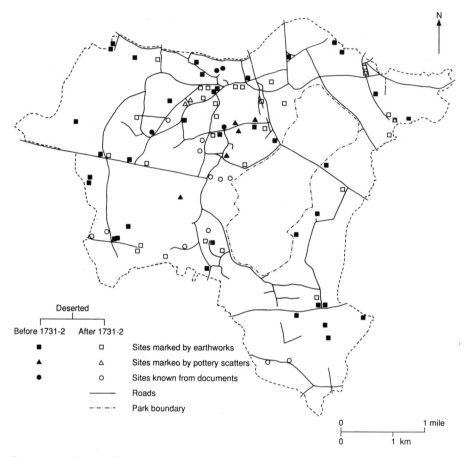

Figure 13   Deserted settlements, 1350–1984.

scale desertion of villages in regions of 'old' settlement, like the Warwickshire Feldon or the Yorkshire Wolds.

A more detailed investigation of the deserted settlements reveals the often complicated social and economic changes that lie behind an apparently simple thinning of surplus messuages. First, the high-status settlements seem to have been as vulnerable as any to the general contraction. The main manor house had fallen out of use as a dwelling for the bishop and his household by the mid-thirteenth century. The agricultural buildings and accommodation for visiting officials which were still in active use in the 1380s became obsolete in 1407 when the demesne was leased out in parcels, and the centralized manorial complex no longer served any useful purpose.[13] At some time the rectory also moved to a site on glebe land below Church Hill. Occupation ceased at *Holeway* grange by 1400; in 1364 *Knottenhull* was exchanged by the monks for a parish church at Kinver (Staffordshire), and the Crown united the land with the Park, as is shown on the map of 1591.[14] The gentry residences seem to have fared better, and all except Park Hall are still inhabited, though there may have been breaks in occupation, for example when Hamburys was taken over by the Staffords of Grafton in the early fifteenth century.[15] These examples show that the fragmentation of estates, changes in management and the amalgamation of holdings all had their impact on the decay of settlements.

The peasant holdings were affected by a similar combination of circumstances. It is worth noting that freeholdings had a rather longer life than customary tenements. In Table 4 we can see that in 1410 the proportion of tofts, compared with messuages, was markedly low on freeholdings.[16]

Table 4   Messuages and tofts in 1410

	Free		Customary	
Tofts	8	(20%)	17	(53%)
Messuages	33	(80%)	15	(47%)
TOTAL	41	(100%)	32	(100%)

This confirms the evidence of table 3, because the majority of the freeholdings were located in the greens, and most of the customary messuages lay in the ends. The freeholdings were on average smaller, and the occupiers cultivated land arguably of inferior quality; but they paid lower rents, their holdings lay nearer to their houses in enclosed crofts, and above all they were free. This gave the tenants practical advantages, in that they could use and abuse their buildings as they wished, fell trees on their holdings, and generally be exempt from petty seignorial restrictions. There were no bad memories for them of marriage fines, *leyrwites* (fines for sexual incontinence) and the other personal humiliations of servile status. Thomas Elvyns typifies the prevailing attitude when, in 1377, he was reported to have both a free and a customary tenement, but he had opted to live on the freeholding.[17] The bishop's officials encountered some difficulty in obtaining tenants for the customary half-yardlands. In 1376 25 of them were said to be lying 'in the lord's hands', which meant that they were let out year by year, not on long-term tenancies. When they were able to find more permanent tenants, it was at the cost of reducing the rent from a theoretical 11s per half-yardland (as in 1299) to an average of 8s. Some ill-favoured holdings were let for much less, even as little as 4s 5d. On many West Midland manors lords were able to demand at least a few shillings as entry fines from new tenants, but at Hanbury in the dark days of the 1420s and 1430s the fines were waived or paid nominally in the form of poultry.[18] Many half-yardlands formed part of composite holdings, in which the land was still used but the redundant messuage decayed into a toft.

Rather than dwelling on the decay of the later Middle Ages, we should appreciate that settlement was shifting rather than collapsing, and that we are witnessing one symptom of a restructuring of the agrarian economy. The disappearance of the bishop's house on Church Hill must be balanced by the building of brand-new houses on the demesne in the fifteenth century. The new farmers were granted sections of the demesne to work as large holdings of 50–100 acres. By 1410 the demesne field of the Hay (once called Ruding) was provided with a messuage, and the farmer of Morecroft also built himself a house near his share of the demesne. The lands of *Holeway* grange were split between two farmers in the late fifteenth century, and one of the tenants, William Hunt, built a house described as 'new' in 1530, on the site of Stonehouse Farm.[19] The division of the demesnes provided one source of lands for substantial tenant farms. More commonly successful cultivators accumulated large holdings by putting together a number of formerly separate tenements. Prominent among these were the gentry and larger freeholders, who began with the advantages of capital and expertise in managing large units of production. When William Wybbe, esquire, died in 1446 he was in possession of no less than eight freeholdings, and he had recently held a ninth. The buildings had collapsed on five of the tenements, judging from the fact that they were called tofts. His total holding must have exceeded 200 acres, and merely to pay his heriots (death duties) a small herd of seven cattle were driven away for the lord's use.[20] There were other prospering élite families at this time, such as the Bearcrofts of Mereplace, and outsiders such as the Staffords of Grafton. Customary tenants could unite holdings to make larger landed units as well: Thomas Bayly had 3 half-yardlands in 1466, and in 1506 John Menske died and bequeathed to his son Thomas 4 half-yardlands and a croft.[21]

The increase in the size of farms – to a point where families would have had difficulty in working them with household labour – was accompanied by changes in agricultural methods. The balance shifted from arable to pasture which required fewer hands. Demand in the market moved from grain to meat, which stimulated stock-farming among both small and large producers. Demesne fields were described as pastures: Buryfield and Morecroft on the bishop's manor, and Down Field and Brook Field at *Holeway* accounted for at least 400 acres of former arable put down to grazing.[22] Parts of tenant holdings were rented out by the administrators of the bishop's manor as pasture. Much tenant land was called leys, which could mean either permanent pasture or temporary grassland in a system of 'convertible' husbandry. In pursuit of new agricultural methods tenants sought to exclude their neighbours from their closes, and were then accused in the manor court of illicit enclosure. Finally in 1539 large-scale enclosure involving 23 tenants and well over 200 acres of land was agreed with the encouragement of the bishop.[23] While tenants nibbled away at the edges of the open fields by exchanging strips, consolidating lands, and then enclosing them, others were upsetting the conventional systems of cultivation, thereby provoking by-laws against those who ignored the old rotation, and who committed breaches of the rules by ploughing up the balks between strips.[24]

The large-scale and individualistic style of the late medieval farming corrects a gloomy view of the period as one of unrelieved decline. New building to some extent offset the loss of some of the old messuages. We have already noted the new farmhouses on the demesnes. Towards the end of the fourteenth century a dozen purprestures were paying rents to the bishop's manor, two at least of which had houses built on them.[25] Some of these enclosures from the waste were very small: in many cases they were strips of roadside verges enclosed as paddocks and cottage sites. But one reported in 1384 measured as much as 11 perches by 11 perches, or about ¾ acre.[26] They represent a continuation of the assarting campaign, and are significantly concentrated in the areas of former colonization, such as Blickley. This extension of settlements continued after 1400, when a new cottage was built at Mere Green in 1452 and a cottage was put on a new assart at Goosehill in 1463.[27] A significant revival of clearance and enclosure of the waste came in 1495, when John Mathew took 'a parcel of waste land lying on the common pasture at Wodrewegrene' and similar grants were being made of new assarts at Blickley in the early sixteenth century.[28] Woodland settlement was never static. New lands were being enclosed and new houses built, even as old assarts lapsed back into the common, and the buildings on the old messuages fell down.

The landlord's role in all this was by no means a decisive and commanding one. In choosing to divide the demesne and to thereby create new farms his officials were probably responding to local pressure, as a single farmer might have been reluctant to take on such a large and unwieldy collection of lands. In the fifteenth century the court made rather ineffective attempts to force tenants to repair their buildings, and in the long run, in the interest of maintaining at least a modest income from rents, the engrossing activity of the better-off tenants had to be accepted. The bishop insisted on receiving a nominal rent when tenants made new encroachments on the common, and Bishop Latimer, in an unusual intervention in the affairs of the manor in 1539, encouraged further enclosure. In all of these cases the impetus and the initiative came from the tenants, and the lord sensibly swam with the tide of events.

The new landscape of the later Middle Ages, with fewer messuages and more enclosure, was linked with the emergence of a new social order. In the late thirteenth century Hanbury's hierarchy consisted of two church estates, that of the bishop and the monks, a handful of gentry and large freeholders, and many middling peasants. The tax list of 1275 covers the whole vill and is based on valuation of goods, of which a fifteenth part was paid in tax. The bishop's wealth towered over that of every other taxpayer: his payment of 36s (representing goods worth £27) no doubt involves a gross under-assessment.[29] Next came the wealthiest of the gentry, Geoffrey de Hambury, who paid 20s (his goods were valued at £15). Nine other people contributed between 4s 6d and 7s 0d (goods worth £3 7s 6d to £5 5s 0d), and the mass of the taxpayers, 67 in all, were assessed at between 1s and 4s 0d (15s 0d to £3). This can be contrasted with the muster of 1522, which assessed the taxable value of both lands and goods.[30] It netted a similar number of people, 87, compared with 78 who paid tax in 1275. As the population had halved, the sixteenth-century assessment must have included a much larger proportion of the inhabitants, which could mean either that Henry VIII's government was much more ruthless than Edward I's in forcing the poor to contribute, or that fewer people were so lacking in resources that they were exempted. Again at the apex was the bishop whose rents were assessed at £25 (a low but not entirely unrealistic figure), together with ecclesiastics who were not included in the earlier tax: Bordesley Abbey (lands worth £50), the rector (lands worth £20 and goods a little more) and the knights of St John, the heirs of the Templars. A few gentry appear, like Humphrey Stafford, esquire, with lands valued at £10, but the remarkable feature is the dozen people with goods valued at £7 to £14 (and one with goods worth £60), and another dozen with goods worth £5 to £6. They form a substantial group, differentiated from the majority who had either lands valued at 6s 8d to 10s 0d, or goods worth between £1 and £2. Some of the middle band of inhabitants were newcomers, but many bore names that had been current in Hanbury for a century or two, like Bearcroft, Cook, Menske and Nashe. They can be identified as engrossers of tenant holdings, like William Bayly and William Yate, and with those who took on large leaseholds, such as Lewes Skargill and William Hunt, the farmer of *Holeway* grange, whose goods were judged to be worth £60. Direct comparison between these lists made 250 years apart is dangerous, but we can observe the emergence by 1522 of a moderately prosperous yeomanry.

The yeomen farmers continued in the long term to dominate the social evolution of Hanbury. The Vernon estate, which grew to take over the bishop's manor and substantial parts of Broughton and *Holeway* as well, had 29 tenant farms in 1731-2, and this number dwindled to 18 in 1840. The average farm on the estate increased from 86 to 167 acres.[31] This should be compared with the 160 or so landholdings in the high Middle Ages, with an average size of below 25 acres. In recent times the amalgamation of holdings has continued. During the 1980s at least three farms were in a ruinous state and two sets of farm buildings have become redundant. There have been periods when new farms were built, for example when the Park was broken up for agricultural land in the seventeenth century, and at the same time the woods in northern Hanbury were felled.[32] But this has had remarkably little effect on the landscape, and the former Park and the 'Forest' can still be identified by their large, straight-edged fields and lack of houses. The pattern of settlement has moved its centre of gravity towards the centre of the parish. One element within this process has been the growth of a ribbon development along Woolmere Green (paralleled by a similar line of cottages at Stock Green) which resemble the encroachment on the wastes and road-sides recorded in the later Middle Ages. Another factor has been the abandonment of houses at Goosehill and Blickley and above all in the ends since 1731-2 (see fig. 13), which has left the western part of the centre of the parish, once the area where a high proportion of the medieval population lived, relatively empty.

The growth of Woolmere Green and the more intensive development of Woodrow, together with the building of the Vernon Arms, gave the central road junction a semblance of a village centre by the time of the tithe map in 1840.[33] More recently the 'village' has acquired an estate of council houses, and local facilities such as a post-office, shop and garage, and Hanbury now has a nucleated settlement which it lacked for the first four millennia of its history.

Chapter 5

Conclusion

Every local example chosen for historical research will have its own peculiarities. Hanbury's importance as an administrative and religious centre in the Iron Age and the early Middle Ages, and its links with Droitwich, mean that it cannot be regarded as typical. However, much of its everyday history resembles that of other woodland communities, and we can extract from it some general lessons.

At the beginning we must express awe at the achievement of prehistoric farmers, who occupied so much land in so many regions, including those clay soils of the Midlands that were once supposed to be uninhabitable. Gradually we are overcoming our prejudices about primitive and backward people, which led us wrongly to assume that societies at an early stage of technical development would be restricted in the scale and location of their settlements. The almost total exploitation of the countryside in the Roman period is becoming almost a commonplace of such local studies, but the quantity of evidence is still impressive. Seen in this light, the people of the Middle Ages do not appear as great initiators, but were following in the footsteps of the real pioneers. In many ways medieval colonizers were simply recovering lost ground, because they were clearing not virgin forest but woods that had regenerated in the post-Roman period.

This leads us to a conclusion about the origins of the *pays* of the Middle Ages. In other parts of the country, particularly in East Anglia, the survival of the boundaries of prehistoric or Romano-British field systems even into modern times has suggested that agrarian life has continued from one period to another.[1] Of course, this does not mean that methods of farming or the organization of the landscape have remained unchanged. In the case of Hanbury the abundance of Roman settlements and cultivated land makes it very unlikely that the place had a woodland character in, say, the second century. Perhaps other woodland landscapes of the Middle Ages can be traced back to the Roman period.[2] But Hanbury, along with many other medieval woodlands, developed its distinctive balance of land use and method of exploiting resources through the regeneration of woods between 400 and 1066, and the subsequent assarting campaigns.

The Hanbury survey lends little support to the simpler theories of continuity, because few medieval farmsteads stand on sites occupied in the Roman period, and the notion that the 'villa estate' evolved into the medieval manor is difficult to apply to a region which lacks villas. And yet the persistence of settlement in western and south-eastern Hanbury, and the successive use of Church Hill as an administrative and cult centre over more than two thousand years provide some support for the idea that peasants and élites alike continued to use the resources of the area. A fruitful line of inquiry surely lies in the similarities between Roman and medieval settlement patterns, both of which were dispersed in separate farmsteads. This cannot be a case of continuity as some of the medieval assart settlements were established after a gap of eight centuries, but it might suggest that in different periods similar solutions were found for the problems of organizing productive agrarian units.[3]

The devolution of the great estate into smaller lordships recorded at Hanbury in the ninth century is exceptional only in the quality of its documentation. We are witnessing in this process not just a change in the boundaries of estates, but a transformation from a tribute-collecting regime to the more intense manorial system based on the linked exploitation of a demesne and peasant obligations. Manors and peasant communities had a complex and interactive relationship.[4] Hanbury was a viable manor in the ninth century, even when shorn of its outlying dependencies, but new manors could not be taken out of its territory until the fringes had acquired a peasantry capable of providing an income for a lord. Lords were rarely given an empty patch of land on which to live, but they may have received a thinly populated area and then encouraged its further colonization. The correlation between the distribution of nucleated villages and the regions where powerful lords wielded most influence has prompted the theory that villages were organized and planned by their lords. Hanbury is not alone in having as its lord a rich and powerful ecclesiastic who had controlled the place from an early date, and whose dependents included many slaves and serfs; and yet it failed to be formed into a nucleated village.[5] The lesson is clear. Lordship did not provide the crucial impetus for nucleation of settlement; the environment mattered much more. Nucleated villages and dispersed settlements were elements within their *pays*, and to explain variations in the form of settlements we need to explore differences in the use and organization of land.

The complex patterns of regional landscapes cannot be given a single deterministic explanation. If soils and climate were all important, how do we explain the boundary between woodland and champion that runs to the south of Hanbury, which coincides with no marked difference in terrain or relief? To reduce the problem to a single example, why did Himbleton, also an ecclesiastical lordship, develop into a nucleated village with a fully fledged open-field system, while Hanbury did not? Population may form part of the background, as the champion parts of the West Midlands were generally more densely peopled than the woodlands, but this would not apply in the specific case of Himbleton, which had even fewer peasants than Hanbury in the eleventh century, and in the awkward case of East Anglia very high populations lived in areas of dispersed settlement.[6] To old notion that the settlement types varied with the ethnic origin of the inhabitants, with Anglo-Saxons living in villages and the British in hamlets, is now discredited: the distribution of villages and of densest Anglo-Saxon settlements bear slight resemblance to one another. The assumption is sometimes made that the dispersed settlements belong to some earlier phase of social evolution. They represent the survival of the early medieval settlement pattern into the high Middle Ages. In the early stages of the Hanbury survey the idea emerged that the 'ends' with their attachment to the open fields represented an embryonic village which never realized its potential: the population failed to reach the critical point needed for nucleation. Again the East Anglian example argues against this view because the densities of population exceeded those of the champion countries. We have to accept that in adjoining districts medieval people lived according to different rules and adopted different ways of life. They developed a range of methods of organizing their farming activities. Regions diverged, but that does not make one more primitive or another more advanced.

We can exaggerate the contrasts between *pays*, and we need to be more aware of the subtle variations within the same type of *pays*. Hanbury had only some of the classic characteristics of a woodland settlement. Many of its peasants were customary half-yardlanders, whose land lay in open fields under common control. The village community had considerable authority in the regulation of the open fields, the common meadows and pastures, and to some extent of the enclosed crofts. The settlements did not ramble aimlessly over the parish, but were organized into coherent groupings, which medieval people called ends and greens, and which we can classify as 'interrupted rows'. The settlements worked as part of an agrarian system, which had a different balance between public and private assets than that which prevailed in the champion districts. A greater emphasis on pasture prevailed in some periods, but not much in the late thirteenth century when a high proportion of the available land had fallen under the plough. Hanbury did not belong to a completely separate species of settlement and landscape. Woodland and champion districts were closely related.

Woodland settlements worked rather well. They were more robust than their neighbours in the champion. Contrary to the extreme notions of continuity, Hanbury's peasants and lords in the thirteenth century embarked on a large-scale campaign of colonization; and in this they were not alone.[7] They extended cultivation onto soils which were probably somewhat inferior to those which had been occupied since the Roman period. Yet, when the retreat came in the later Middle Ages, the new assarts were not always the first to be abandoned. Just as in the national scene the deserted villages are found in areas of old and continuous settlement, a high proportion of Hanbury's desertions were in the western ends. The crises exposed the vulnerability of the villages of the champion, where the delicate social balance of the village community and the closely regulated fields suffered such a shock that in the many cases they collapsed completely.[8] The woodlands were more resilient. They cannot be regarded as suffering from Malthusian pressure of population nor were social burdens so oppressive. The peasants were not bound together in such close mutual dependence, and a half of the inhabitants could disappear without irreparable damage to the whole system. Already in the late fourteenth and fifteenth centuries we can identify the beginnings of a new phase in the history of the woodlands, in which farms merged into larger units of production, and labourers' cottages spread on the greens.

Abbreviations

AHR	*Agricultual History Review*
BAR	British Archaeological Reports
CPR	*Calendar of the Patent Rolls*
CS	*Cartularium Saxonicum*, ed. W. de Gray Birch (3 vols, 1885–91)
DB	*Domesday Book*, Record Commission (1783)
EcHR	*Economic History Review*
HWCRO	Hereford and Worcester County Record Office (Worcester branch)
LA	Liber Albus of the bishopric of Worcester, HWCRO, ref. 821 BA 3814
PRO	Public Record Office
PRS	Pipe Roll Society
RBW	*Red Book of Worcester*, ed. M. Hollings, WHS (4 parts, 1934–50)
Talbot	Calendar of the Manuscripts relating to Worcestershire contained in the Shrewsbury (Talbot) Collection, deposited in the British Museum (Birmingham Reference Library, 1937)
VCH	*Victoria County History*
WHS	Worcestershire Historical Society

Notes

Chapter 1. Introduction

1. H.P.R. Finberg, *Roman and Saxon Withington: a Study in Continuity*, University of Leicester Dept. of English Local History, Occasional Paper, 1st ser., 8 (1957); M. Spufford, *A Cambridgeshire Community: Chippenham from Settlement to Enclosure*, University of Leicester Dept. of English Local History, Occasional Paper, 1st ser., 20 (1965); C. Phythian-Adams, *Continuity, Fields and Fission: the Making of a Midland Parish*, University of Leicester Dept. of English Local History, Occasional Paper, 3rd ser., 4 (1978); B. Schumer, *The Evolution of Wychwood to 1400: Pioneers, Frontiers and Forests*, University of Leicester Dept. of English Local History, Occasional Paper, 3rd ser., 6 (1984); K.J. Allison, M. W. Beresford, J.G. Hurst *et al.*, *The Deserted Villages of Oxfordshire*, University of Leicester Dept. of English Local History, Occasional Paper, 1st ser., 17 (1965); K.J. Allison, M.W. Beresford, J.G. Hurst *et al.*, *The Deserted Villages of Northamptonshire*, University of Leicester Dept. of English Local History, Occasional Paper, 1st ser., 18 (1966).
2. C. Fox, *The Personality of Britain* (1932).
3. O. Rackham, *The History of the Countryside* (1986).
4. A. Everitt, 'River and wold: reflections on the historical origins of regions and *pays*', *Journal of Historical Geography*, 3 (1977), 1–19; J. Thirsk, *Agricultural Regions and Agrarian History in England, 1500–1700* (1987), 37–55.
5. R.H. Hilton, *Social Structure of Rural Warwickshire in the Middle Ages*, Dugdale Soc. Occasional Paper, 9 (1950); J.B. Harley, 'Population trends and agricultural developments from the Warwickshire Hundred Rolls of 1279', *EcHR*, 2nd ser., xi (1958–9), 8–18; J.B. Harley, 'The settlement geography of early medieval Warwickshire', *Trans. Institute British Geographers*, 34 (1964), 115–30; B.K. Roberts, 'A study of medieval colonisation in the Forest of Arden, Warwickshire', *AHR*, 16 (1968), 101–13; B.K. Roberts, 'Field systems of the west midlands', in *Studies of Field Systems in the British Isles*, ed. A.H.R. Baker and R.A. Butlin (1973), 188–231; C. Dyer, *Warwickshire Farming 1349–c.1520*, Dugdale Soc. Occasional Paper, 27 (1981).
6. Schumer, *op. cit.*, 11–16; M.W. Beresford, *The Lost Village of England* (1954); C.J. Bond, 'Deserted medieval villages in Warwickshire and Worcestershire', in *Field and Forest. An Historical Geography of Warwickshire and Worcestershire*, ed. T.R. Slater and P.J. Jarvis (1982), 147–71. On the changing character of *pays* see H.S.A. Fox, 'The people of the wolds in English settlement history', in *The Rural Settlements of Medieval England*, ed. M. Aston, D. Austin and C. Dyer (1989), 77–101.

7. These issues are raised by G.C. Homans, *English Villagers of the Thirteenth Century* (1941), 111–219; R.H. Hilton, 'Old enclosure in the west midlands: a hypothesis about their late medieval development', in R.H. Hilton, *Class Conflict and the Crisis of Feudalism* (1985), 36–47; T. Williamson and L. Bellamy, *Property and Landscape* (1987), especially 29–53.

8. M.W. Beresford and J.G. Hurst (eds), *Deserted Medieval Villages* (1971); C.C. Taylor, *Village and Farmstead* (1983).

9. G. Cadman and G. Foard, 'Raunds, manorial and village origins', in *Studies in Late Anglo-Saxon Settlement*, ed. M.L. Faull (1984), 81–100; D. Austin, *The Deserted Medieval Village of Thrislington, County Durham. Excavations 1973–74*, Soc. for Medieval Archaeology Monograph, 12 (1989), 164–7.

10. B.K. Roberts, *Rural Settlement in Britain* (1977), 15–17.

11. Aberrant villages: J.G. Hurst, 'The Wharram Research Project: results to 1983', *Medieval Archaeology*, 28 (1984), 77–111.

12. P. Wade-Martins, 'Village sites in Launditch Hundred', *East Anglian Archaeology*, 10 (1980), 17–75; P. Warner, *Greens, Commons and Clayland Colonization*, University of Leicester Dept. of English Local History, Occasional Paper, 4th ser., 2 (1987); M. Aston, 'Deserted farmsteads on Exmoor and the lay subsidy of 1327 in west Somerset', *Somerset Archaeology and Nat. Hist.*, 127 (1983), 71–104; H.S.A. Fox, 'Peasant farmers, patterns of settlement and *pays*: transformations in the landscapes of Devon and Cornwall during the later middle ages', in *Landscape and Townscape in the South-West*, ed. R. Higham (1989), 41–73; M.L. Faull and S.A. Moorhouse (eds), *West Yorkshire: an Archaeological Survey to AD 1500* (4 vols, 1981), III, 585–613; D. Austin, 'The excavation of dispersed settlements in medieval Britain', in Aston *et al.* (eds), *op. cit.*, 231–46.

13. T.H. Aston, 'The origins of the manor in England', *Trans. Royal Hist. Soc.*, 5th ser., viii (1958), 59–83, reprinted with a postscript in *Social Relations and Ideas*, ed. T.H. Aston, P.R. Coss, C. Dyer and J. Thirsk (1983), 1–43; G.R.J. Jones, 'Multiple estates and early settlements', in *Medieval Settlement*, ed. P.H. Sawyer (1976), 15–40.

14. P.D.A. Harvey, 'Initiative and authority in settlement change', M. Aston *et al.* (eds), *op. cit.*, 31–43.

15. S. Reynolds, *Kingdoms and Communities in Western Europe, 900–1300* (1984).

16. E.g. C. Dyer, 'Deserted medieval villages in the west midlands', *EcHR*, 2nd ser., xxxv (1982), 19–34.

17. C. Dyer, *Lords and Peasants in a Changing Society. The Estates of the Bishopric of Worcester 680–1540* (1980).

18. *Ibid.*, 94–5.

19. G. Baseley, *The Archers. A Slice of my Life* (1971), 49.

20. M.W. Beresford and J.G. Hurst, *Wharram Percy* (1990); B. Cunliffe, 'Saxon and medieval settlement-pattern in the region of Chalton, Hampshire', *Medieval Archaeology*, xvi (1972), 1–31; Cadman and Foard, *op. cit.*

21. B.S. Smith, 'The Dougharty family of Worcester, estate surveyors and mapmakers, 1700–60', in *Miscellany II*, WHS, new ser., 5 (1967), 138–77.

22. *VCH Worcs.*, III, 58.

23. B. Cunliffe, *Iron Age Communities in Britain* (1974), 100–3.

24. A.H. Smith, 'The Hwicce', in *Franciplegius: Medieval and Linguistic Studies in Honour of Francis Peabody Magoun, Jr*, ed. J.B. Bessinger and R.P. Creed (1965), 56–65; H.P.R. Finberg, *The Early Charters of the West Midlands* (1961), 167–80; D. Hooke, *The Anglo-Saxon Landscape: the Kingdom of the Hwicce* (1985); S. Bassett, 'In search of the origins of Anglo-Saxon kingdoms', in *The Origins of Anglo-Saxon Kingdoms*, ed. S. Bassett (1989), 6–17.

25. Dyer, *Lords and Peasants, op. cit.*, 75.

26. D. Freezer, *From Saltings to Spa Town* (1977).

27. F.T.S. Houghton, 'Salt-ways', *Trans. of the Birmingham Archaeological Soc.*, liv

(1929–30), 1–17; D. Hooke, 'The Droitwich salt industry; an examination of the west midland charter evidence', in *Anglo-Saxon Studies in Archaeology and History*, 2, BAR, British ser., 92 (1981), 123–69.

28. *RBW*, pt 2, 182–3.
29. HWCRO, ref. 705: 7 BA 7335/38.
30. Freezer, *op. cit.*; J. Crickmore, *Romano-British Urban Settlements in the West Midlands*, BAR, British ser., 127 (1984), 74–5.
31. M. Aston, 'Earthworks at the bishop's palace, Alvechurch, Worcestershire', *Trans. Worcs. Archaeological Soc.*, 3rd ser., 3 (1970–2), 55–61; C.C. Taylor, 'Somersham Palace, Cambridgeshire: a medieval landscape for pleasure?', in *From Cornwall to Caithness*, ed. M. Bowden *et al.*, BAR, British ser., 209 (1989), 222–3.
32. Hanbury, like the other episcopal manors, was a jurisdictional peculiar exempt from the powers of the archdeacon: *VCH Worcs.*, III, 379.
33. J.M. Ragg *et al.*, *Soils and their Use in Midland and Western England*, Soil Survey of England and Wales, Bulletin 12 (1984), 156–9, 190–3, 319–23, 327–9. I am grateful for the advice of Dr S. Limbrey.
34. B. Saward, 'Climate', in *Birmingham and its Regional Setting*, ed. M.J. Wise (1950), 47–54.

Chapter 2. Origins: Until Domesday

1. I am very grateful to Dr L. Barfield for his comments on the flints and the hill-fort.
2. The object was commented on by Mrs E. Proudfoot, Dr A. Saville and Dr D. Simpson, to whom I am grateful; they suggested as parallels F.K. Annable and D.D.A. Simpson, *Guide Catalogue of the Neolithic and Bronze Age Collections in Devizes Museum* (1964), no. 19; C. Scott-Garrett, 'Tidenham Chase Barrow', *Trans. Bristol and Glos. Archaeological Soc.*, lxxiv (1955), 15–35.
3. L.H. Barfield and M. Hodder, 'Birmingham's Bronze Age', *Current Archaeology*, 78 (1981), 198–200; L. Barfield and M. Hodder, 'Burnt mounds as saunas, and the prehistory of bathing', *Antiquity*, 61 (1987), 370–9.
4. F.W. Shotton, 'Archaeological inferences from the study of alluvium in the Lower Severn–Avon Valleys', in *The Effect of Man on the Landscape: the Lowland Zone*, ed. S. Limbrey and J.G. Evans, Council for British Archaeology Research Report, 21 (1978), 27–32.
5. South of Park Farm, at SO 967616. I am grateful to Mr P. Booth for his comments on this sherd.
6. W.A. Cotton, *An Account of Early British and Roman Coins Found at Hanbury, Worcestershire* (1886), 5–6; C.N.S. Smith, 'A catalogue of the prehistoric finds from Worcestershire', *Trans. Worcs. Archaeological Soc.*, xxxiv (1957), plate 2 and p. 26; the more recent finds by metal-detector users include one at SO 953654 described as a Dobunnic quarter stater inscribed CORIO (Glendinning's sale catalogue, September 1983, 15) and two other staters of EISV of gilt copper, found at SO 951644. Information from Mr W.A. Seaby.
7. The lynchets are at SO 953641 (south-west of the church), SO 963643 (in the area now known as the Valley), and at SO 948632 (north of Pumphouse Lane).
8. D. Freezer, *From Saltings to Spa Town* (1977), 1.
9. Information from the Hereford and Worcester County Council Sites and Monuments Record, by courtesy of Mr J.P. Roberts.
10. *Ibid.*, and Cambridge University Aerial Photograph VV50, of a site with twin rectangular enclosures south of Summerhill Farm.
11. Based on the advice of Mr P. Booth and Dr A.S. Esmonde-Cleary.
12. Information from Mr D. Symons of Birmingham City Museum, based on the reports of a metal-detector user in 1980. The finder was vague about which objects

came from the roadside, and which from the area to the south of the road. The identification of the lion is by Mr Symons.

13. I am grateful to Dr D. Mackreth for his advice on this object.

14. S. Johnson, *Later Roman Britain* (1980), 159.

15. P. Salway, *Roman Britain* (1981), 542–4 draws a similar conclusion for the whole province.

16. R. Hingley, *Rural Settlement in Roman Britain* (1989), 97–101; C. Hayfield, *An Archaeological Survey of the Parish of Wharram Percy, East Yorkshire. The Evolution of the Roman Landscape*, BAR, British ser., 172 (1987), 90–5.

17. Hingley, *op. cit.*, 127–8.

18. A.S. Esmonde-Cleary, *The Ending of Roman Britain* (1989), 157–9.

19. P.A. Rahtz, 'Hatton Rock, 1970', *Trans. Birmingham and Warwickshire Archaeological Soc.*, lxxxv (1971-3), 172–4; E. Morris, 'Medieval and post-medieval pottery in Worcester–a type series', *Trans. Worcs. Archaeological Soc.*, 3rd ser., vii (1980), 221–54; A. Vince, 'Did they use pottery in the Welsh Marches and the West Midlands between the 5th and 12th centuries AD?', in *From Roman Town to Norman Castle*, ed. A. Burl, University of Birmingham, Department of Extramural Studies, 1988, 40–55.

20. T. Hearne (ed.), *Hemingi Chartularium Ecclesiae Wigorniensis* (2 vols, 1723), II, 567. The importance of the notes was recognized in H.P.R. Finberg, *The Early Charters of the West Midlands* (1961), 12.

21. On the general problem of the very early charters, P. Chaplais, 'The origin and authenticity of the royal Anglo-Saxon diploma', *Journal of the Soc. of Archivists*, iii (1965-6), 48–61.

22. CS 416; D. Whitelock (ed.), *English Historical Documents I, c. 500–1042* (1958), 477–9.

23. E.g. CS 350; 351; 430.

24. E.g. W.J. Ford, 'Some settlement patterns in the central region of the Warwickshire Avon', in *Medieval Settlement*, ed. P.H. Sawyer (1976), 274–94.

25. CS 22.

26. DB, I, fo. 174; *VCH Worcs.*, III, 397. This is based on a suggestion by Mr S. Bassett, who has usefully discussed the charters with me.

27. N.P. Brooks, *The Early History of the Church of Canterbury* (1984), 175–206.

28. The earliest reference is to *Walemere* in 1328; HWCRO, ref. 705:7 BA 7335/39; the identification was made by M. Gelling. It has subsequently appeared in K. Cameron, 'The meaning and significance of Old English *walh* in English place-names', *Journal of the English Place-Name Soc.*, 12 (1980), 42.

29. P.S. Gelling, 'Report on excavations in Bays Meadow Droitwich, Worcestershire, 1954–5', *Trans. Birmingham Archaeological Soc.*, lxxv (1957), 9; the Upwich dates forthcoming in *Medieval Archaeology*, xxxiv (1990).

30. A. Mawer and F.M. Stenton, *The Place-names of Worcestershire*, English Place-Name Society, iv (1927), 323.

31. CS 76; Hearne (ed.), *op. cit.*, 187–9; A.J. Robertson, *Anglo-Saxon Charters* (2nd edn, 1956), 208–11.

32. Mawer and Stenton, *op. cit.*, 281.

33. DB, I, fos 174, 180. This is based on the assumption that the eleventh-century Park did not change in size during the Middle Ages, and uses the formula in O. Rackham, *Ancient Woodland* (1980), 113–17.

34. This presumes that a demesne plough cultivated 100 acres and a tenant plough 50; see C. Dyer, 'The rise and fall of a medieval village: Little Aston (in Aston Blank), Gloucestershire', *Trans. Bristol and Glos. Archaeological Soc.*, 105 (1987), 170.

35. W.E. Wightman, *The Lacy Family in England and Normandy* (1966), 53.

36. F.J. Monkhouse, 'Worcestershire', in *The Domesday Geography of Midland England*, ed. H.C. Darby and I.B. Terrett (1954), 24.

37. *Holeway* was granted to the Cistercian abbey of Bordesley in about 1140. It was therefore exempted from tithe, and it continued as a tithe-free area until the

commutation of 1840. For the general point of exemption, C. Platt, *The Monastic Grange in Medieval England* (1969), 57–61. The tithe-exempt area on the Hanbury tithe map of 1840 (HWCRO, ref. x 760/314 BA 1572) defines the area of the early Cistercian acquisition. The extensions of the thirteenth century were covered by an agreement of 1238 by which Bordesley paid the rector of Hanbury 20s. p.a.: PRO, E326/B11831.

38. Finberg, *op. cit.*, 103.
39. G.W.S. Barrow, *The Kingdom of the Scots* (1973), 8–68.
40. C. Dyer, *Lords and Peasants in a Changing Society* (1980), 28–30.
41. The first detailed description is *RBW*, pt. 2, 186–8, but they must have been in existence by the time of Domesday.
42. D.C. Douglas (ed.), *English Historical Documents 2, 1042–1189* (1953), 814.
43. S.P.J. Harvey, 'Taxation and the ploughland in Domesday Book', in *Domesday Book. A Reassessment*, ed. P.H. Sawyer (1985), 95–6.
44. G. Duby, *Early Growth of the European Economy* (1974), 227–56.
45. DB, I, fos 172–3.
46. A cartload of wood for a mitt seems to have been a standard exchange: DB, I, fo. 172 (Bromsgrove); 173 (Northwick).

Chapter 3. Hanbury in its Prime: Eleventh to Fourteenth Century

1. A. Everitt, *Continuity and Colonization. The Evolution of Kentish Settlement* (1986); J.S. Moore, *Laughton: A Study in the Evolution of the Wealden Landscape*, University of Leicester Dept. of English Local History, Occasional Paper, 1st ser., 19 (1965); D.M. Palliser, *The Staffordshire Landscape* (1976), 70–6.
2. M. Aston, *Interpreting the Landscape* (1985), 86–90; M. Bell, 'Environmental archaeology as an index of continuity and change in the medieval landscape', in *The Rural Settlements of Medieval England*, ed. M. Aston, *et al.* (1989), 269–86.
3. B. Schumer, *The Evolution of Wychwood to 1400: Pioneers, Frontiers and Forests*, University of Leicester, Dept. of English Local History, Occasional Paper, 3rd ser., 6 (1984), 14 and 57.
4. The sources for the table are DB, I, fos. 174, 180; *RBW*, pt 2, 171–84, 186–8. *Holeway* seems not to have been depopulated by the creation of the Cistercian grange. A gang of seven men who committed a trespass against the earl of Pembroke in 1319 (*CPR, 1317–21*, 369), included a Richard de Holeway. The population of Broughton is estimated on the basis that twelve people appear from there in the muster of 1522 (PRO, E36/35). For the assumption that Domesday slaves might have families, see J. Moore, 'Domesday slavery', *Anglo-Norman Studies*, xi (1988), 191–220.
5. Examples in Worcestershire are Alvechurch, C. Dyer, *Lords and Peasants in a Changing Society* (1980), 85; and Pendock, C. Dyer, 'Dispersed settlements in medieval England. A case study of Pendock, Worcestershire', *Medieval Archaeology*, xxxiv (1990), forthcoming. Elsewhere, see H.E. Hallam (ed.), *The Agrarian History of England and Wales*, II (1988), 537–84.
6. J.R. Birrell, 'Medieval agriculture', in *VCH Staffs*, VI, 7.
7. *RBW*, pt 2, 187. On the general problems of the period, E. Miller, 'England in the twelfth and thirteenth centuries: an economic contrast?', *EcHR*, 2nd ser., xxiv (1971), 4–5.
8. *RBW*, pt 4, 435.
9. *VCH Worcs.*, III, 377; I.J. Sanders, *English Baronies* (1960), 94.
10. *RBW*, pt 2, 186.
11. H.A. Cronne and R.H.C. Davis (eds), *Regesta Regum Anglo-Normannorum* (4 vols, 1913–69), III, 42–3; *Rotuli Litterarum Clausarum*, Record Commission (2 vols, 1833–44), I, 417.
12. PRS, new ser., iv (1927), 66–9; J.W. Willis Bund (ed.), *Inquisitions Post Mortem for the*

County of Worcester, pt 1, WHS (1894), 4. A parker's estate is mentioned in the Bordesley foundation charter, cited in the previous note.

13. The bishop was reported by a forest jury for a house in a purpresture, probably at Blickley, in Henry III's reign, PRO, E146/3/3; *RBW*, pt 2, 185.

14. PRS, i (1884), 23; xvi (1893), 98; new ser., i (1925), 5; new ser., ii (1926), 84; new ser., vi (1929), 57.

15. The contribution to the bishop's revenues is calculated from Dyer, *Lords and Peasants, op. cit.*, 53.

16. *RBW*, pt 2, 186-8.

17. *RBW*, pt 2, 149-50; pt 4, 422-3; L. Landon, *Cartae Antiquae Rolls 1-10*, PRS, new ser., xvii (1939), 75-6.

18. J. West, 'The administration and economy of the Forest of Feckenham during the early Middle Ages' (M.A. thesis, University of Birmingham, 1964), 336-8, 349-51.

19. PRO, E32/227; 229; 232; 319; *RBW*, pt 2, 172, 175.

20. LA, fos 57, 60-1, 65.

21. LA, fos 43-4, 62.

22. *RBW*, pt 2, 180-1.

23. *Rotuli Parliamentorum*, Record Commission (6 vols, n.d.), I, 198; Worcester Cathedral Priory, Liber Albus of the Priory, fos xxix^v, lxi^v, ciii^v; R.A. Wilson (ed.), *The Register of Walter Reynolds, Bishop of Worcester, 1308-1313*, Dugdale Soc., ix (1928), 35, 43; E.H. Pearce (ed.), *The Register of Thomas de Cobham, Bishop of Worcester, 1317-1327*, WHS (1930), 9; Talbot, 38.

24. *Rotuli Hundredorum*, Record Commission (2 vols, 1812-18), II, 284-5; *RBW*, pt 2, 172; PRO, E32/229; *Calendar of Inquisitions Miscellaneous*, III, 181.

25. LA, fos 59-60; *RBW*, pt 2, 172-3; Bishop Blois (1218-36) bought an assart at Stocking, LA, fo. 62.

26. PRO, E32/229.

27. For similar behaviour elsewhere, E. King, *Peterborough Abbey 1086-1310* (1973), 99-125; Z. Razi, *Life, Marriage and Death in a Medieval Parish. Economy, Society and Demography in Halesowen 1270-1400* (1980), 50-5. For the Wynter sisters, *RBW*, pt 2, 175.

28. LA, fos 59-60, 60-1.

29. PRO, E32/229.

30. N. Pevsner, *The Buildings of England, Worcestershire* (1968), 184.

31. J.W. Willis Bund (ed.), *Register of Bishop Godfrey Giffard*, WHS (1898-1902), 311; *RBW*, pt 2, 173.

32. HWCRO, ref. 705:7 BA 7335/39; ref. 009:1 BA 2636/166, nos 92237 and 92254.

33. PRS, v (1885), 56; vii (1886), 4; xi (1889), 64; xiii (1890), 177, and subsequent references in the same series show works on ponds and buildings at Feckenham. The ponds were almost certainly those in the Park, and the buildings could well have included the lodge: H.M. Colvin, *History of the King's Works* (7 vols, 1963-82), II, 937-8. The farmhouse, recently demolished, contained old timbers that could have come from the medieval lodge: comments by Mr A. Harris.

34. Talbot, 48-9.

35. The site was first drawn and interpreted by Mr M. Aston, who kindly supplied copies of his notes.

36. PRO, SC6/Henry VIII, 7444.

37. On moats as status symbols, see F.A. Aberg (ed.), *Medieval Moated Sites*, Council for British Archaeology Research Report, 17 (1978), 46-8.

38. *CPR, 1232-47*, 18.

39. HWCRO, ref. 009:1 BA 2636/167 no. 92299 (in 1446 the vill of Broughton was ordered not to occupy the road on the Hanbury side of the boundary). Broughton made presentments both to the bishop's view of frankpledge, and to the swanimotes of Feckenham Forest: R.H. Hilton (ed.), 'Swanimote rolls of

Feckenham Forest', in *Miscellany I*, WHS (1960), 37–52.

40. The evidence of building types comes from the court rolls: a barn of four bays in 1444, HWCRO, ref 009:1 BA 2636/167 no. 92296; a barn of three bays in 1455, R.K. Field, 'Worcestershire peasant buildings, household goods and farming equipment in the later middle ages', *Medieval Archaeology*, ix (1965), 135. Henry Sherard agreed to build a bakehouse on a messuage in Goosehill in 1463: HWCRO, ref. 009:1 BA 2636/168 no. 92328. In 1410–11 another holding at Goosehill had three buildings constructed on it: HWCRO, ref. 705:7 BA 7335/37.

41. The maps are HWCRO, ref. f. 970.5:7 BA 1101/1; Brit. Lib., Maps, P 12609: M1 6 b1(12). Especially likely to be new buildings are the roadside cottages, e.g. on the Roman road toward Droitwich, and Summerhill Farm in western Hanbury.

42. It might be thought that the Park would have been closed to travellers, and indeed the diversion of the roads around it might suggest that at one time it had been totally enclosed. In 1502 there appears to have been a fenced 'high road' between Feckenham gate and Hanbury gate: Hilton (ed.), *op. cit.*, 48.

43. B.K. Roberts, *The Making of the English Village* (1987), 33–62.

44. Deeds of 1305 and 1340 describe holdings in Blickley that lie between the brook and the bishop's wood: Talbot, 37, 45. For parallels see P. Warner, *Greens, Commons and Clayland Colonization*, University of Leicester, Dept. of English Local History, Occasional Paper, 4th ser., 2 (1987), 29–38.

45. Talbot, 66; Geoffrey and John de Uppington paid taxes in 1275; J.W. Willis Bund and J. Amphlett (eds), *Lay Subsidy Roll for the County of Worcester circ. 1280*, WHS (1893), 33.

46. A group of three tenements at Huntingdrop is described in a deed of 1388, HWCRO, ref. 705:7 BA 7335/34.

47. D. Dymond and E. Martin (eds), *An Historical Atlas of Suffolk* (2nd edn, 1989), 70–1.

48. C.C. Taylor, *Village and Farmstead* (1983), 151–74; P.D.A. Harvey (ed.) *The Peasant Land Market in Medieval England* (1984).

49. D. Pelteret, 'The *coliberti* of Domesday Book', *Studies in Medieval Culture*, 12 (1976), 43–54.

50. *RBW*, pt 2, 171–3. Both compact and dispersed demesnes are found in champion villages: D. Hall, 'Fieldwork and field-books: studies in early layout' in *Villages, Fields and Frontiers*, ed. B.K. Roberts and R.E. Glasscock, BAR, International ser., 185 (1983), 117–18.

51. PRO, SC6/Henry VIII, 7444.

52. HWCRO, ref. 721:091 BA 2358/5, no. 38.

53. For Hamburys, Talbot, *passim*, and Brit. Lib., Add. Roll 74158; for Wybbes, Society of Antiquaries of London, Prattinton Colln, vol. XVII, fo. 277.

54. HWCRO, ref. 009:1 BA 2636/166 no. 92269.

55. HWCRO, ref. 009:1 BA 2636/168 no. 92332.

56. HWCRO, ref. 009:1 BA 2636/167 no. 92279; *RBW*, pt 2, 175.

57. B.K. Roberts, 'Field systems of the west midlands', in *Studies of Field Systems in the British Isles*, ed. A.H.R. Baker and R.A. Butlin (1973), 209–18, 226–30; V.H.T. Skipp, 'The evolution of settlement and open-field topography in north Arden down to 1300', in *The Origins of Open Field Agriculture*, ed. T. Rowley (1981), 162–83.

58. HWCRO, ref. 009:1 BA 2636/9 no. 43696, fos 28r–30r.

59. HWCRO, ref. 705:7 BA 7335/65.

60. For similar examples, J. Thirsk, 'The common fields', in *Peasants, Knights and Heretics*, ed. R.H. Hilton (1976), 20–2.

61. Talbot, 66.

62. HWCRO, ref. 705:7 BA 7335/64, 65; ref. 009:1 BA 2636/169 no. 92356.

63. HWCRO, ref. 705:7 BA 7335/65; ref. 705:192 BA 5589/82.

64. Brit. Lib., Maps, P 12609: M1 6 b1(12); on compartmented parks, O. Rackham,

Ancient Woodland (1980), 195.

65. Hilton (ed.), *op. cit.*, 50; Rackham, *op. cit.*, 193.
66. PRS, xxvii (1906), 55. The estimate of numbers presumes a payment of 1d or ½d per pig.
67. HWCRO, ref. 705:7 BA 7335/39; ref. 009:1 BA 2636/165 no. 92225²/₈.
68. HWCRO, ref. 009:1 BA 2636/168 no. 92319;/169 no. 92353.
69. *Calendar of Inquisitions Miscellaneous*, III, 181; the woods of the other manors as mentioned in the forest records (PRO, E 146/3/4) and in the account of *Holeway* at the time of the Dissolution, when *Holeway* had a 'common wood' (PRO, SC6/Henry VIII, 7444).
70. *RBW*, pt 2, 173.
71. HWCRO, ref. 705: 7 BA 7335/64.
72. HWCRO, ref. 009:1 BA 2636/167 no. 92281.
73. For the twelfth century, see the PRS references in note 14 above; for 1393-4, PRO, E 364/31; the ponds are planned and discussed in M. Aston and C.J. Bond, 'Worcestershire fishponds', in *Medieval Fish, Fisheries and Fishponds in England*, ed. M.A. Aston, BAR, British ser., 182 (1988), 437-42.
74. J.M. Steane, 'The royal fishponds of medieval England', in Aston (ed.), *op. cit.*, 39-68.
75. *RBW*, pt 2, 171-4, 184-6; *Calendar of Inquisitions Miscellaneous*, III, 181; Society of Antiquaries of London, Prattinton Colln, vol. XVII, 271.
76. For example, the bishop's pasture for 300 sheep in 1299 could be regarded as equivalent to 50 acres.
77. HWCRO, ref. 009:1 BA 2636/168 no. 92315.
78. This composite picture depends on many sources, but especially important depictions of woodland society are J. Thirsk (ed.), *The Agrarian History of England and Wales*, IV (1967), 111-12; G.C. Homans, *English Villagers of the Thirteenth Century* (1941), 109-20; J.R. Birrell, 'Peasant craftsmen in the medieval forest', *AHR*, 17 (1969), 91-107; R. Hilton, *A Medieval Society. The West Midlands at the End of the Thirteenth Century* (2nd edn, 1983), 241-8.
79. R.M. Smith, 'Human resources', in *The Countryside of Medieval England*, ed. G. Astill and A. Grant (1988), 198-202.
80. PRO, E 146/3/3.
81. Dyer, *Lords and Peasants, op. cit.*, 321.
82. HWCRO, ref. 009:1 BA 2636/165 no. 92229.
83. PRO, E 32/319.
84. Dyer, *Lords and Peasants, op. cit.*, 101, 108.
85. Hilton, *op. cit.*, 109-10.
86. The evidence of smithing at Wyntors came to light when a pipe-trench was dug across the field in 1979. The work was observed by D. Hutton.
87. R. Holt, *The Mills of Medieval England* (1988), 30, 166-7.
88. Hilton, *op. cit.*, 175-6.
89. Dyer, *Lords and Peasants, op. cit.*, 346-9, 368.
90. Dr A. Vince kindly identified the source of the medieval pottery found in field-walking. A chapman from Shropshire sold stolen lambs in Hanbury in 1431: HWCRO, ref. 009:1 BA 2636/167 no. 92275.
91. Dyer, *Lords and Peasants, op. cit.*, 301-4. The figures exclude land passing to widows.

Chapter 4. Settlement Retreat, and New Beginnings

1. On the large number of shrunken villages, C.J. Bond, 'Medieval Oxfordshire villages and their topography: a preliminary discussion', in *Medieval Villages*, ed. D. Hooke (1985), 101-23.
2. A. Preston-Jones and P. Rose, 'Medieval Cornwall', *Cornish Archaeology*, 25 (1986),

146–51; M. Bailey, *A Marginal Economy. East Anglian Breckland in the Later Middle Ages* (1989), 309–19; C.F. Tebbutt, 'A deserted medieval farm settlement at Faulkners Farm, Hartfield', *Sussex Archaeological Collections*, 119 (1981), 107–16; P.V. Addyman, W.G. Simpson and P.W.H. Spring, 'Two medieval sites near Sedbergh, West Riding', *Yorkshire Archaeological Journal*, xli (1966), 27–42.

3. J. Hatcher, *Plague, Population and the English Economy 1348–1530* (1977); R.M. Smith, 'Human resources', in *The Countryside of Medieval England*, ed. G. Astill and A. Grant (1988), 191.

4. C. Dyer, *Lords and Peasants in a Changing Society* (1980), 240.

5. PRO, E36/35; T.R. Nash, *Collections for the History of Worcestershire* (2 vols, 1781–2), I, 548.

6. The neo-Malthusian view is expounded in M.M. Postan, *The Medieval Economy and Society* (1972), and is discussed in T.H. Aston and C.H.E. Philpin (eds), *The Brenner Debate* (1985).

7. *VCH Worcs.*, IV, 470.

8. Z. Razi, *Life, Marriage and Death in a Medieval Parish* (1980), 45.

9. Dyer, *op. cit.*, 79.

10. *Ibid.*, 223.

11. HWCRO, ref. 009:1 BA 2636/168 no. 92332.

12. M. Bailey, 'The concept of the margin in the medieval English economy', *EcHR*, 2nd ser., xlii (1989), 1–17; C. Dyer, '"The retreat from marginal land": the growth and decline of medieval rural settlements', in *The Rural Settlements of Medieval England*, ed. M. Aston *et al.* (1989), 45–57.

13. HWCRO, ref. 705:7 BA 7335/37.

14. *CPR, 1361–4*, 438–9.

15. Talbot, 70–1.

16. HWCRO, ref. 009:1 BA 2636/9 no. 43696, fos 28–9.

17. HWCRO, ref. 009:1 BA 2636/166 no. 92232.

18. Dyer, *Lords and Peasants, op. cit.*, 288–9; B.F. Harvey, *Westminster Abbey and its Estates in the Middle Ages* (1977), 271.

19. HWCRO, ref. 009:1 BA 2636/9 no. 43696, fo. 28ʳ (the Hay). The Morecroft evidence is archaeological; for *Holeway*, a tithe dispute of *c.* 1530 records the division of the demesne and the new house: PRO, E 328/25/1,2,3,6,7.

20. HWCRO, ref. 009:1 BA 2636/167 no. 92299.

21. HWCRO, ref. 009:1 BA 2636/168 no. 92332; ref. 705:7 BA 7335/64.

22. HWCRO, ref. 009:1 BA 2636/167 no. 92276; PRO, SC6/Henry VIII 7444.

23. Dyer, *op. cit.*, 333–5.

24. HWCRO, ref. 009:1 BA 2636/169 no. 92363; ref. 705:7 BA 7335/64.

25. HWCRO, ref. 009:1 BA 2636/166 no. 92254.

26. HWCRO, ref. 009:1 BA 2636/166 no. 92247.

27. HWCRO, ref. 009:1 BA 2636/167 no. 92309; ref. 705:7 BA 7335/65.

28. HWCRO, ref. 705:7 BA 7335/64, 65. The same phenomenon of new settlements in the time of retreat has been noted by A.J.L. Winchester, *Landscape and Society in Medieval Cumbria* (1987), 48–51.

29. J.W. Willis Bund and J. Amphlett (eds), *Lay Subsidy Roll for the County of Worcester circ. 1280*, WHS (1893), 33–4.

30. PRO, E 36/35; see J.C.K. Cornwall, *Wealth and Society in Early Sixteenth Century England* (1988), especially pp. 165–71, and for criticisms of the reliability of these documents, R.W. Hoyle (ed.), *Early Tudor Craven: Subsidies and Assessments 1510–1547*, Yorks. Arch. Soc. Record Ser. cxlv (1987), xiv–xix.

31. J. Yelling, *Common Field and Enclosure in England, 1450–1850* (1977), 119, 128.

32. J. Amphlett (ed.), *A Survey of Worcestershire by T. Habington*, WHS (2 vols, 1895–9), I, 253–4.

33. HWCRO, ref. x 760/314 BA 1572.

Chapter 5. Conclusion

1. W. Rodwell, 'Relict landscapes in Essex', in *Early Land Allotment*, ed. H.C. Bowen and P.J. Fowler, BAR, British ser., 48 (1978), 89–98.
2. It has been suggested that the distribution of Roman tile and pottery kilns in parts of north Warwickshire and west Worcestershire reveal the presence of abundant wood fuel in those districts: G. Webster, 'Prehistoric settlement and land use in the west midlands and the impact of Rome', in *Field and Forest. An Historical Geography of Warwickshire and Worcestershire*, ed. T.R. Slater and P.J. Jarvis (1982), 49.
3. R. Hingley, *Rural Settlement in Roman Britain* (1989), 97–101.
4. The problem has caused debate from the early years of scientific history, e.g. P. Vinogradoff, *Villainage in England* (1892), 397–409.
5. The presence of church estates in abundance in the champion areas, but also extending into the woodland, is shown by J. Hamshere, 'Domesday Book: estate structures in the west midlands', in *Domesday Studies*, ed. J.C. Holt (1987), 166–71.
6. T. Williamson, 'Explaining regional landscapes: woodland and champion in southern and eastern England', *Landscape History*, 10 (1988), 5–13.
7. E.g. H.E. Hallam, *Settlement and Society* (1965); M. Williams, *The Draining of the Somerset Levels* (1970); H.E. Hallam (ed.), *The Agrarian History of England and Wales*, II (1989), 176–7, 180–7, 254–5, 267–8.
8. C. Dyer, 'Deserted medieval villages in the west midlands', *EcHR*, 2nd ser., xxxv (1982), 19–34.